WRESTLING WITH COLONIALISM

ON STEROIDS

"A Political History of Nunavik" is based on a series of weekly radio commentaries broadcast on CBC North.

The first version of "Wrestling With Colonialism on Steroids" was written in 2013 and spurred the making of the documentary film *Napagunnaqulusi: So That You Can Stand*, released on the 40th anniversary of the signing of the James Bay and Northern Quebec Agreement, in 2015.

Wrestling with Colonialism on Steroids

QUEBEC INUIT FIGHT FOR THEIR HOMELAND

Zebedee Nungak

WITH A FOREWORD BY
TAGAK CURLEY

Véhicule Press

Published with the generous assistance of the Canada Council for the Arts, the Canada Book Fund of the Department of Canadian Heritage, and the Société de développement des entreprises culturelles du Québec (SODEC).

Canadä   SODEC Québec ⊞ ⊞

 Canada Council   Conseil des arts
for the Arts   du Canada

Dossier Québec
Cover design: J.W. Stewart
Typeset in Minion and Filosofia by Simon Garamond
Photos, unless indicated otherwise, courtesy of Zebedee Nungak
Author cover photo courtesy of Avataq Cultural Institute
Cover background photo by FargomeD, Creative Commons license
Special thanks to William Tagoona and Ole Gjerstad
Printed by Marquis Printing Inc.

LIBRARY AND ARCHIVES CANADA CATALOGUING IN PUBLICATION

Nungak, Zebedee, 1951-, author
Wrestling with colonialism on steroids :
Quebec Inuit fight for their homeland /
Zebedee Nungak ; foreword by Tagak Curley.

(Dossier Québec series)
Issued in print and electronic formats.
ISBN 978-1-55065-468-4 (softcover). – ISBN 978-1-55065-476-9 (EPUB)

1. James Bay Hydroelectric Project. 2. Inuit – Québec (Province)–
Government relations. 3. Inuit – Land tenure – Québec (Province).
4. Inuit – Colonization – Québec (Province). 5. Inuit – Québec (Province) – History. 6. Nunavik (Québec) – History. I. Title. II. Series:
Dossier Québec series

E99.E7N857 2017   971.4'115004971   C2016-907366-1
C2016-907367-X

Distributed in Canada by LitDistCo
Distributed in the U.S. by Independent Publishers Group

Printed in Canada on FSC certified paper.

CONTENTS

Zebedee Nungak on Parliament Hill, 1965.

[TOP] Zebedee in Puvirnituq, 1960s.
[BOTTOM] With son William, Kangirsuk, 1975.

FOREWORD

Over the last 50 years, our destiny as Inuit has evolved in remarkable, challenging, and at times uncertain ways, to say the least. Governments and other non-Inuit authorities responsible for Inuit well-being and Arctic policy had little respect and understanding of the issues that affected our lives in our land. Serious dialogue was almost non-existent.

During those critical times Inuit began to rise up. They formed their own organizations, developed leadership, and began to speak out. In this book, Zebedee Nungak takes us through the historical context and eloquently portrays how things changed dramatically when the Government of Quebec and the provincial utility Hydro-Québec began construction of the massive James Bay hydro-electric project. The government proceeded without any consideration or consultation with Quebec's Inuit and Cree, whose hunting grounds would be flooded and otherwise affected by the project. There was no consideration of environmental questions, never mind aboriginal rights to the land. The Cree and Inuit were faced with an urgent need to be heard, but neither group had any organization ready and able to represent them.

Zebedee, who at the time was a young public servant working for the Federal Government, tells of meeting with Charlie Watt, an Inuk mechanic at George River. At that time, in the early 1970s, I was a young civil servant working for the Northwest Territories Government. But I was fortunate to be a part of the early leadership developments of our national Inuit organization. The Inuit Tapirisat of Canada, ITC, was formed in 1971 when Inuit from all across the regions gathered in Pangnirtung for the founding meeting. I was elected as its National President. For the first time Inuit established a unified voice in Canada. ITC established its head quarters in Ottawa, and the office became a strategic location whenever our regional groups would arrive for meetings with the Federal Government.

The James Bay hydro project and the plight faced by the Inuit and Cree were regularly covered on CBC Radio national and regional news. It was evident that in Northern Quebec, Inuit were caught between a rock and a hard place. Who would fight for their cause? Then I learned that they were represented by the Indians of Quebec Association, so I wrote a personal letter to "the mechanic" at George River, Charlie Watt, urging him and the Québec Inuit to form their own organization. Soon after, a series of meetings resulted in the formation of the Northern Quebec Inuit Association, the NQIA. It had members from every Inuit community. Its leaders were astute and dedicated, and included some colorful personalities. They set the agenda. Charlie Watt was elected President. Zebedee, still a young Inuk, was educated and fluent in Inuktitut and English. He was born an orator and with a memory sharper than a harpoon. This exciting break-through is rendered in fascinating detail in this book. The overall story Zebedee tells is encouraging to all of us who are interested in public life; he tells us to continue to fight, at every level of our lives in our land.

As I read this book, I am reminded that Inuit life, manifested by our history of survival as a unique people rooted in our land, is full of opportunity. We have learned to stand together and fight when faced with uncertainty and adversity, however complex. That strength comes through on every page in the story, as told by Zebedee Nungak. He brings in the context of the battle for the Canadian Constitution and the evolution of a more progressive Confederation. I can assure you that reading this Inuit version of a chapter of Canadian history will be an eye-opener, particularly with respect to our relations with provincial and federal governments. It is also good preparation for land claims discussions still to come.

Tagak Curley
Rankin Inlet, July 2016

Long, Rough Osmosis

A Political History of Nunavik

PART 1

Quebec Discovers "Nouveau-Québec"

Recently, as I was interviewed about Nunavik history by two different filmmakers, it became apparent that many basic facts about Nunavik's evolution are barely known. The first obvious fact, almost totally missing from people's consciousness, is this: Nunavik has not always been part of Quebec. And further, once Quebec acquired the Ungava District of the Northwest Territories (the future Nunavik) in 1912, the Quebec government was totally absent from the territory for more than five decades.

Colonial acts of European monarchs, and then legislation of successive post-colonial "immigrant" governments, triggered a series of events that resulted in Quebec eventually "discovering" Arctic Quebec. Its name changed from Rupert's Land to Ungava District of the NWT, then to Nouveau-Quebec, and finally to Nunavik. To short-circuit the historical timeline, Quebec gained jurisdiction over this territory in 1912, when my grandfather Tulugak was a 13-year-old boy.

Fifty-two years later, in 1964, I myself was 13 when Quebec government officials first arrived in what they called Le Grand Nord. A political awakening in southern Quebec, known as the Quiet Revolution, caused Liberal Premier Jean Lesage to dispatch his Minister of Natural Resources north. René Lévesque went to Fort

Premier Jean Lesage sent Minister of Natural Resources
René Lévesque north to meet with Inuit leaders, 1964.
*Photo by J.-A. Quirion, courtesy of Avataq Cultural Institute
and Éric Gourdeau Fonds.*

Chimo to meet with Inuit leaders to declare Quebec's
intention to be present "forthwith" in the 1912 lands.

The new rulers came north with an attitude of "We're
the Bosses here now!" This didn't sit well at all with many
of the Inuit leaders who met with Minister Lévesque. The
late Jacob Oweetaltuk, then an outspoken young man,
pointedly asked Lévesque: "In all those years, when you
were knowingly the government of this land, why didn't
you erect an outpost, even the size of an outhouse, somewhere here?"

Far from being embarrassed by its 52-year absence,
Quebec officialdom went on a nationalistic bender of
misguided Québécois patriotic pride. It named the territory "Nouveau-Québec", although it had been Quebec

In Fort Chimo, Jacob Oweetaltuk (right) asked René Lévesque: "In all those years, when you were knowingly the government of this land, why didn't you erect an outpost, even the size of an outhouse, somewhere here?"

since 1912. The only thing "nouveau" in the nationalism-charged atmosphere was Quebec's delightful infatuation with all this land, *which they only discovered now!* Quebec was like a big kid, fascinated with a shiny, wondrous new toy.

An agency called the Direction générale du Nouveau-Québec (DGNQ) was established to administer services parallel to those already provided by the federal government. Before long, its inept governing style earned it the catchy nickname, "Don't Go Near Quebec". That moniker gained currency when the government turned its attention to our northern place names.

"Poste-de-la-Baleine" to
"Port Nouveau-Québec"

Starting in 1964, Quebec imposed French names on the Inuit communities. They also did this for prominent points of geography, which already had names in Inuktitut and in English. The practitioners of "featherweight colonialism" were determined to concoct a French identity for the 1912 lands.

Kuujjuaraapik, called Whapmagoostui in Cree and Great Whale River in English, was transformed into Poste-de-la-Baleine. Many Inuit could only manage a phonetic approximation of the new name. Port Harrison, Inukjuak, was designated the spelling of Inoucdjouac – Inuktitut with a very francized spelling. People weren't expected to mind this too much, it at least being the French phonetic approximation of Inukjuak.

Povungnituk was not changed at all, not even francized in spelling, a mystery of the whims and imagination of those responsible for formulating this new set of names. It changed years later to Puvirnituq, by its residents' fiat, as it should be. But Ivujivik became Notre-Dame-d'Ivugivik – Our Lady of Ivugivik. On the new map, the 'N' in Notre started way out at sea, very close to Southampton Island, for the 'k' in Ivugivik to coincide with the dot on the map.

Sugluk a.k.a. Salluit, became Saglouc. Wakeham Bay a.k.a. Kangiqsujuaq became Maricourt. I've been told that it was actually Sainte-Anne-de-Maricourt, but I have never seen that name on the map. Kangiqsujuaq has become closest to reclaiming its old English name, by sheer popular usage of Wakeham Bay. Koartak became Notre-Dame-de-Koartac, another "Our-Lady-of" designation. Payne Bay a.k.a. Kangirsuk, became Bellin. A knowledgeable source once told me he had seen it as Bellin-sur-Mer, but I have never seen this suffix.

Leaf Bay a.k.a. Tasiujaq, became Baie-aux-Feuilles. Tommy Cain Sr., a prominent leader of that community, once told me that he stopped resenting this concocted French name only when he was sleeping. Fort Chimo, Kuujjuaq, got off lightly, by simply being given a hyphen between its two words. This was another mystery of the unfathomable whims of Quebec's name revisers. But it was now pronounced "Fore-SheeMoe".

George River a.k.a. Kangiqsualujjuaq became Port-Nouveau-Québec. Cape Weggs a.k.a. Nuvujjuaq, between Salluit and Kangiqsujuaq, became Cap de Nouvelle-France. Chubb Crater a.k.a. Pingualuit became Cratère du Nouveau-Québec. Cape Jones a.k.a Tikirarruaq, at the edge of James and Hudson Bays, became Pointe-Louis-XIV. All these names were arbitrarily dictated by Quebec, without any notice or consultation with Nunavimmiut.

Governed by Eager Amateurs

The name Quebec has only two syllables, but Inuit don't have one standard pronunciation of it. Different locations in Nunavik have slightly different variations of saying the word, as they do with all newly encountered matters. The concept and substance of Quebec does not at all exist in Inuit traditions. It's often spoken with the suffix, *-kut,* meaning "those of": *Kupaikkut, Kipaikkut, Kupiakkut, Kupaakkut,* and sometimes colloquially as *Ouigouikkut* (those French ones).

In the early 60s, a song composed by Jobie Arnaituk was very popular: "Taitsumani Inuit sivullivuulli" (Long ago, our Inuit ancestors) Around the late 1960s, after Quebec had "governed" the north for a few years, somebody added a refrain to this song: "Kupaikkut sunaqanngitut, Tamaanii-laujunnginamik; Kisiani maannaapik tikilauramik, Sinnaatumaanngitulluuniit!" Those of Quebec have absolutely nothing! No wonder! They've never been here previously. They've arrived so recently, they don't have a clue (about what on Earth to do!)

What Quebec did have plenty of was eagerness to prove its governing credibility through the very odd means of duplicating activities of the northern federal administration. Quebec's mindset seemed to be: "If somebody else has been *governing* this part of 'our' land, we've got to get busy to do exactly as they're do-ing!" The new provincial bureaucracy, DGNQ, started issuing provincial family allowances, welfare payments, and many other things.

Mindless duplication of government services was the order of the day, and went on for about a decade. The barely 4,000 people of Nunavik were entangled in layers of over-administration by two levels of govern-ment, without being directly represented provincially or federally.

Federal day schools with English-only curriculum already existed. But Quebec set up a parallel school system under an entity called the Commission scolaire du Nouveau-Quebec (CSNQ), a school board without elected commissioners created especially for the region by Order-in-Council. Along with instruction in French, CSNQ offered the unique novelty of instruction in Inuk-titut by Inuit teachers. That was at least one hit among a lot of misses.

Maps of Quebec were very interesting, and not only for their proud display of newly minted French geo-graphical names. Some maps didn't show the Labrador boundary, so Quebec appeared much larger than it actu-ally was. Nationalism, awakened by the Quiet Revolu-tion, tried its best not to recognize the 1927 decision of the British Privy Council, which had delineated the Labrador border. Being governed by eager amateurs pretending to disregard the realities of long-defined boundaries was interesting enough, but we had yet to encounter the mind-bending phenomenon of Quebec separatists.

The 1912 Law – Designed by Pure Colonialism

The first foreign colonial act which blanketed Inuit ancestral lands was the Royal Charter issued by King Charles II of England on May 2, 1670. Although it was the height of pretension for English superiority, the charter didn't contain anything overtly pernicious toward the rights of Aboriginal people. The land simply became the king's "Rupert's Land", named after his cousin. Even the Act creating the Northwest Territories in 1870 did not yet articulate any deadly legal hoops that would shackle and complicate Aboriginal rights.

The 1912 legislation, which transferred Inuit ancestral lands from the Northwest Territories to Quebec, is called, "An Act respecting the extension of the Province of Quebec by the annexation of Ungava". It was passed on April 3, 1912 and is only three pages long. It is usually referred to as The Quebec Boundaries Extension Act. At the time, Robert Borden, a Conservative, was Prime Minister of Canada, and Lomer Gouin, a Liberal, was Premier of Quebec.

The impact of this law would forever change the lives of Nunavik Inuit; it was the work of pure colonialism. Its meandering preamble states: "…the Parliament of Canada may, from time to time, with the consent of the Legislature of any Province, increase, diminish or otherwise alter the limits of such Province, upon such terms and conditions as may be agreed to by said Legislature and may, with like consent, make provision respecting the effect and operation of any such increase, diminution or alteration of territory".

What a revelation it is that the Parliament of Canada can diminish or otherwise alter the limits of Provinces! Why doesn't federalism ever wield this lethal sledgehammer toward Quebec separatists during referendums?

The design of this 1912 Act was a blueprint for governments forcing subservience on Inuit subjects, and the legal formula requiring Aboriginal surrender was to destroy Inuit harmony in 1974 when we negotiated the James Bay and Northern Quebec Agreement (JBNQA). Section 2 (c) states: "That the province of Quebec will recognize the rights of the Indian inhabitants in the territory above described to the same extent, and will obtain surrenders of such rights in the same manner, as the Government of Canada has heretofore recognized such rights and has obtained surrender thereof, and the said province shall bear and satisfy all charges and expenditure in connection with or arising out of such surrenders".

In 1974, during the dark moments of the JBNQA negotiations, the federal and provincial governments wielded this legislative noose from 1912 as an absolute, non-negotiable condition, requiring Aboriginal people to "surrender and extinguish their rights in and to the lands" being negotiated over. As we found out, the future of Inuit unity was already doomed in 1912.

Unnatural Osmosis

Nunavik being part of Quebec is a continuous long, rough, unnatural osmosis. When the land transfer deed was enacted by federal legislation in April 1912, many points of natural law were greatly violated. Here are some of them:

There were no hearings where Aboriginal occupants of these lands could voice objections to this real estate deal between governments. Our great-grandfathers had no chance to insist on anti-separatism provisions, which would automatically revert the territory back to Canada if Quebec separation were ever pursued.

Aboriginal occupants of these lands were not notified, let alone consulted, about this third change in their status as citizens of yet another jurisdiction. We had been involuntary Rupert's Landers since 1670, and Northwest Territorians since 1870. Now our ancestral lands were annexed to Quebec, Canada's most problematic jurisdiction, snuffing out a common future with fellow Inuit in Nunavut.

There were no surveys of Canada's gift to Quebec. Whoever drew Saskatchewan's boundaries in 1905 was not around to simply draw a huge rectangle. The post-colonial governments set the high-water mark as the boundary, surely without assessing how insanely squiggly this boundary is.

Quebec failed to immediately send its officials to take inventory of who, and what, was in their new acquisition. There was not yet a Canadian Prime Minister whose stated policy for Arctic lands was, "Use it or lose it!" The 1912 transfer would have been a real test case for such an approach.

By not seeking Inuit consent, Canada failed to exercise its fiduciary responsibility to protect their interests. This responsibility was clearly stated in section 91 (24) of the British North America Act, 1867. But recognition of the "existing" rights of Aboriginal people was still seventy years away, and the Supreme Court decision called Tsilqhot'in was 102 years away.

In 1936, 24 years after gaining jurisdiction over these lands, Quebec refused to pay for welfare provided to Inuit by the Hudson's Bay Company during the Depression of the 1930s. Quebec formally pleaded in Supreme Court that Inuit were none of its business! It argued emphatically that its Inuit citizens were "Indians", and therefore Canada's responsibility. In other words: The land, yes; the people, no!

The Supreme Court handed down its decision regarding the constitutional status of Canada's Inuit (Re: Eskimo SCR 104) in 1939. Quebec won its legal battle with Canada, and that decision has never been overturned. Somewhere out in the legal ether of Canada and Quebec we are still "Indians", patched onto a jurisdiction we would never willingly choose to be part of.

Lock, Stock, and Federal Caretaker

When Canada gave away the Ungava District of the Northwest Territories to Quebec in 1912 the transfer appeared to be a complete deal – lock, stock, and barrel. All the land which encompassed the future Nunavik was placed formally in the realm of provincial government jurisdiction. As such, Quebec should have gotten busy establishing its provincial *bona fides* in the territory without having to worry about federal constraints and distractions.

However, the Supreme Court decision of 1939 complicated the thrust of the deal. Quebec refused to pay the cost of welfare for the Eskimos living in the lands it had acquired 27 years earlier. Canada's government was forced to maintain responsibility for the existence of Quebec Inuit. For instance, Canada operated Royal Canadian Mounted Police (RCMP) detachments in three locations in the region: Port Harrison (Inukjuak) from 1936 to 1961, Great Whale River (Kuujjuaraapik) from 1940 to 1959, and Fort Chimo (Kuujjuaq) from 1942 to 1961. These were the only on-the-ground government agencies in Arctic Quebec until the 1950s, when they were augmented at disparate times with Northern Administrators and federal schools in some of the larger settlements.

As a result, Arctic Quebec was administered exactly like the Inuit communities of the Northwest Territories (later Nunavut), by the federal Department of Northern Affairs and National Resources (D.N.A. & N.R.). The federal government, having lost the Supreme Court "Eskimo" case, didn't have much choice except to provide family allowance, welfare, and old age pensions to Inuit. It conducted censuses and issued Eskimo Identification discs – the (in)famous E-9 and E-8 tags.

Canada provided the first rudimentary housing for the Inuit of Nunavik: one-room slant-walled "Anorak's" and "Match-Box 370s" (based on square footage), with bathtub but no running water. Later came 3-bedroom bungalows which seemed the very lap of luxury. Canada established Community Councils, albeit consultative bodies without formal powers and no budgets. It kick-started development of co-operatives, and ran the economic start-up Eskimo Loan Fund.

In short, Quebec was utterly absent from this territory until 1964. This should have been a case of "use-it-or-lose-it". In all that time, the only overt thing residents could associate to being in Quebec was their mailing addresses: Povungnituk, Que., Fort Chimo, Quebec, Sugluk, Que., and so on. Quebec owes a debt of gratitude to Canada for having taken up the slack in providing government services to residents of the former Ungava District.

Maîtres Chez Nous

Quebec's arrival in the Arctic was charged with francophone nationalist energy, which included a phrase proclaiming the prevailing attitude of its political elite: *maîtres chez nous*. These words, translated as "masters of our own house", didn't sound particularly contentious. In fact, there's nothing odd about collectives of people adopting such self-affirming slogans. Naturally, we all want to be "masters of our own house", and to be our own bosses!

However, in the context of French history in Quebec, this politically-loaded statement implies that those subscribing to it had never been their own bosses before, or were somehow oppressed by others. But let us take a step back and recall that the French are recent arrivals in North America – Quebec City, their first permanent settlement on Canada's shores, was established in 1608. The Inuit of Nunavik, by contrast, out-occupy the French here by about 3,600 years, based on carbon-dating science!

Had they established proper relationships with First Nations in the vicinity of Samuel de Champlain's first colony, they could have been *maîtres chez nous* of whatever areas of land they attained in treaty with Aboriginal nations. Later on, they should surely have been *maîtres chez nous* of the land aptly named *Nouvelle France.* Colonial history is peppered with wars between kingdoms and nations, interspersed with treaties, whereby lands changed colonial "owners" quite frequently.

Any *maîtres chez nous* previously possessed by the French in Quebec was dramatically shattered in a battle, on the Plains of Abraham on the outskirts of Québec City. This occurred when the British defeated the French in September 1759. Just the mention of this date, and the place where this happened, still darkens the countenances of French descendants, 258 years after the fact. The memory of military defeat is hard to shake off.

The French eventually regained some measure of *maîtres chez nous* in Lower Canada, whose population was predominantly French, at the time of Canada's establishment in 1867. Nobody would much question the *maîtres* part of this slogan if only Quebec's boundaries had been confined to the areas where Champlain's descendants lived and farmed, there to maintain and nurture their distinct French identity, language, and culture to their heart's content. The problem crops up in the *chez nous* part, which eventually included *Eeyou Estchee* (Cree Land) and *Inuit Nunangat* (Inuit Land), particular stretches of geography with not a single iota of French history, language, and culture in them. These should not have been bundled in with the French *chez nous.* But that is exactly what happened when Quebec charged ahead with the James Bay Project.

Inuit Negotiate
the James Bay Agreement

A Story to Be Told

Every year on Remembrance Day, November 11th, the anniversary of the signing of the James Bay and Northern Quebec Agreement struggles to be noted as a sideline asterisk on the same day as the solemn honoring of those who have been killed in war. But forty-some years after this agreement was signed, the hard-luck character of the JBNQA gains poignancy by being forced to share the somber emotions of the recollection and reverence of the war dead.

A few Remembrance Days ago I did some public reminiscing on the signing of that Agreement. One of the points I made was that we actually signed the darned thing past midnight. So, although the date of November 11th appears on the document, it was technically November 12th when the 27 signatories wrote their names on their designated lines, and made history.

The main reason for the delay was that its contents were being negotiated literally up to and beyond the last minute of midnight, November 11, 1975. This detail has never been exposed very much, but I would swear to it in a written affidavit because I was there. My signature is one of the names on page 454. Others who were there that day can confirm this fact.

The original target signing date had been November 1, 1975. But with so much unfinished business, there was no hope of concluding by that deadline. So we went to Ottawa to seek a ten-day extension in negotiations. Sam Silverstone, a lawyer who still works for the Makivik Corporation, clearly remembers this. Sam and I were part of a delegation sent to meet Dr. Robert Holmes, a Conservative opposition MP, who was instrumental in getting us this delay.

The consequences of the JBNQA have resulted in reactions ranging from unjustified praise, which would have its producers fast-tracked to sainthood, to unadorned hatred that would have them hung high in the town square. The truth lies somewhere in the middle and has to be discovered through first-hand stories from the surviving veterans who were there. We have to tell our stories while we are still alive.

Extreme Colonialism on Steroids

On June 8, 1576, three ships under the command of Martin Frobisher departed England on a voyage that would reach southern Baffin Island. Queen Elizabeth I is said to have waved from a window to convey her good wishes to the expedition. It is certain that those good wishes did not include formal instructions to Frobisher to secure all relevant permissions and licenses from local Eskimos before proceeding with any mining venture on their lands.

This colonial oversight, we know, was no accident. The pattern of behavior of European monarchs and their successor governments would use such "oversights" down through the centuries to assault and decimate the security and well-being of indigenous people, including Inuit, the world over.

The British legal system has been the single most lethal weapon used to eradicate Inuit sovereignty over Arctic homelands in Canada. There's no room in this system for indigenous oxygen – it was, and still is, utterly foreign to indigenous life. It has built-in superiority over lesser beings not descended from Europeans. No defense against it has ever been discovered, and its effects reign to this day. Present-day governments inherited this extreme colonialism on steroids.

Let's see… In 1670, King Charles II of England issued a royal charter granting his cousin Prince Rupert "ownership" over "Rupert's Land". Our ancestral homelands became the private property of the Hudson's Bay Company. In 1867, Canada was established without any Aboriginal participation. In 1870, Rupert's Land was transferred from the Crown to the new Dominion of Canada. In 1898, Quebec's boundaries were extended to the Eastmain River. In 1912, they were further extended to Ungava District (today's Nunavik).

It took the Province of Quebec 52 years to show up in the lands it gained in 1912. Some strains of colonialism take their own sweet time to get around to examining their acquisitions. In 1964, the Liberals under Premier Jean Lesage were in power in Quebec, and a brash, switched-on Minister of Natural Resources named René Lévesque opened up Le Grand Nord. Quebec's first order of business was to dub the territory "Nouveau-Québec", and francize its community names, as previously discussed.

Colonialism on steroids nurtured certain attitudes that became government tradition, such as "We've been Boss over you even before we came here. You need our permission to run anything important!" This bred a political atmosphere in which governments were automatically superior and Aboriginal people naturally inferior, and this atmosphere prevailed at the time of the James Bay negotiations. These were not friendly talks in the spirit of "Now, let's negotiate the James Bay Agreement!"

"Project of the Century"

When Quebec Premier Robert Bourassa announced his government's initiation of the James Bay hydro-electric project in April 1971, he called it the Project of the Century. For him and those who supported this mega-project, the grandiosity of the enterprise matched any quasi-biblical description. The Cree of James Bay, on whose land this was to happen, were not even notified. There were no hearings. Quebec was playing out its own version of "extreme colonialism on steroids". Not a passing thought was given to the rights of Aboriginal people, although land transfer acts by governments contained specific references to rights, to be dealt with sometime in the unforeseen future. The words "Aboriginal" and "rights" were hardly even in the lexicon of governments of the day. Governments in Canada were not enlightened at all about indigenous people having rights, let alone having roles to play in national and provincial political life.

The federal government had produced a White Paper in June 1969 to fundamentally change the Government-Aboriginal relationship. It proposed to abolish the Indian Act, eliminate the status of the term "Indian", and transfer the responsibility of "Indian affairs" to provinces. The Minister of Indian Affairs at the time, Jean Chrétien, encountered universal resistance from First Nations, who saw the proposal as an attempt to assimilate them into white society.

In Quebec, Bourassa had hatched his plan for the rivers of James Bay in secret meetings with Hydro-Quebec executives just as he was launching his bid to lead the Quebec Liberals after Premier Jean Lesage resigned. He made the development of James Bay hydroelectricity a major plank in his leadership campaign in 1970, and won. He promised prosperity through development of natural resources and jobs, jobs, jobs!

An Inuk elder visiting the NQIA office in Kuujjuaq in 1972 came upon a photograph of Bourassa and studied it in silence for a long time. Then he asked if this was the *angjuqqaaq* (leader) of Quebec, now damming rivers in James Bay. When I answered yes, he said, "His face is too smooth! He doesn't have wrinkles enough to have acquired any wisdom! Be wary of him and his intentions. And don't be afraid to contend with him!"

When Inuit started to confront the James Bay project, negotiating with governments did not seem a possible option. The Project of the Century was barreling full steam ahead, oblivious to any objections. Besides, any attempt to stop it seemed to be a real-life Mission: Impossible!

Rude Political Awakenings

When Robert Bourassa launched the James Bay project, neither the Cree of James Bay nor the Inuit of Northern Quebec had any regional organizations to represent their political interests. Inuit communities only had Community Councils, consultative bodies without formal powers, or budgets, which had been established by the federal Department of Northern Affairs and National Resources. Back then, Inuit leaders were fortunate to get meetings with civil servants holding "Superintendent" titles.

Northern Quebec, known as Arctic Quebec by the federal government, was a quintessential political backwater. Nothing of significance provincially or nationally had yet happened in the vast territory. Even Liberal cabinet minister René Lévesque's visit to Fort Chimo (Kuujjuaq) in 1964 was simply formal notice of Quebec's intention to be present forthwith in "Nouveau-Québec".

The region was populated with just over 4,000 Inuit, living in eleven villages. An oft-mentioned statistic was that all Inuit from the territory could fit into one corner of the Montreal Forum, which could accommodate almost 18,000 people.

When the James Bay project exploded onto the public agenda in 1971, it seemed that nobody in the villages was equipped to tackle the issue collectively for the Inuit.

A rational response and reaction to the project's immense impacts on the region and its people were beyond the grasp of any single leader or entity. The Bosses of government had determined that rivers would be diverted to produce hydroelectricity. Nobody, it seemed, could do anything about that!

Enter the Indians of Quebec Association (IQA), the first indigenous organization to take an interest in the need for Indians and Inuit in Northern Quebec to have political representation. Being Indians, the Cree of Great Whale River were naturally drawn to IQA meetings and activities and quickly became members. Many Inuit Community Council presidents were eager for the IQA to provide them with advice about how Inuit should deal with this issue. Part of the attraction was an Indian leader, Chief Max Gros-Louis, whom Inuit immediately called *Allaaluk qiliqsilialuk* (Big Indian with Braided Hair), who had a reputation as a fearless advocate able to confront governments. What Inuk could better that?

The Inuit of Great Whale River (Kuujjuaraapik) were several steps ahead of Inuit in other communities. Some of them had attended IQA meetings, and most Great Whale Inuit quickly became card-carrying members. One great tangible benefit of IQA membership was enjoying tax exemption for items purchased in stores, simply by flashing that card.

During this period, the Inuit of Northern Quebec existed in a neither-here-nor-there political void.

Uncertainties in a Political Void

The Inuit of Northern Quebec had to find ways and means to speak for themselves in the political arena. When the subject was discussed seriously for the first time, several possibilities quickly surfaced seemingly from nowhere. The dilemma was choosing the right option. For quite a while, it seemed that the best hope was for Inuit to join the IQA as members.

The Cree of Great Whale River had been attending IQA meetings right from around the time the James Bay project became the biggest issue in Quebec. So, in the absence of any other political entity to be part of, the Inuit of Great Whale River had also been drawn to the IQA activities. At the time, there was nothing noticeably unusual about Inuit being members of an Indian organization.

Another element in the atmosphere was a theory that had caught on within the intellects of some Inuit: Arctic Quebec could form a "government" of its own! A delegation of three Inuit men had gone south to meet with senior officials of the Quebec government to discuss local issues and had been told, "You're already a government!" Some people started taking this comment seriously. It seemed to those who subscribed to this rumor-cum-idea that all Inuit had to do was to make a coherent proposition to ask for it and, presto, a government would materialize!

As well, around this time the Fédération des coopératives du Nouveau-Québec (FCNQ), established in 1967, was the source of developing ambitions among their member community co-ops to grow into something much more substantial than retail operations. It was said that the co-ops' corporate structure could facilitate all manner of development. Allegedly, the only exceptions out of bounds to co-ops were health services and railroads. By this logic, Inuit already had a readily existing corporate pathway to pursue their political goals.

In short, Inuit leadership in Northern Quebec had to juggle several distinct political possibilities: First, a significant segment of the Inuit population already held IQA membership. With the community of Umiujaq not yet in existence, Great Whale River was a major Inuit population center. The IQA was a "ready-to-go sled" they could simply jump on. Second, there seemed to be a simple political short-cut available for the asking, to seek the formation of an Inuit "government". Finally, there was yet another remote possibility: forming a representative association for the Inuit of Northern Quebec.

Searching for The Way

Searching for The Way that would serve as the political voice for Northern Quebec Inuit was at times wildly uncertain, but very stimulating. It was sometimes filled with graphic friction among many strong personalities. People who took part in these discussions in the fall of 1971 and early 1972 were not afraid to express themselves, or to strongly disagree with the opinions of others. As a young man in the thick of it, I was awed by the brilliant speeches.

A meeting of Inuit leaders from the then eleven communities was convened in Puvirnituq in September 1971. I was there on the sidelines and don't even recall who chaired the meeting, or by what means delegates got there. This meeting was a rough-and-tumble heated debate among Inuit for the political soul of Northern Quebec. Being on the edge of our own "Challenge of the Century" – the James Bay project – there was no shortage of ideas on how to go about it.

This Great Debate lasted two full weeks. The previously attractive "ready-made salvation" of becoming members of the Indians of Quebec Association quickly evaporated, as the two other options staged a great tug-of-war. Some people advocated simply forming a government for the territory; others wanted to form an association to represent Inuit in the way Indians in the rest of Canada were then doing to great effect, from what we were hearing.

Going for a "government" sounded wonderful and seemed like a ticket into the Big Time. Details such as mandates from constituents to pursue this, and getting the provincial and national governments to be open to discussions weren't of too much concern. Furthermore, this sounded like an ethnic Inuit-only government, which could be used to boss around the Qallunaat for once. Nobody worried about the fine legalities of the "Aboriginal right to self-determination."

Having to invent an Inuit political process was to go where no Eskimo had gone before. Each possibility seemed to be the best way forward for Inuit. Pioneering excitement was in the air. Convincing speakers tried to convert each other. By the end of two weeks, no decision one way or the other had been made. Participants at that *Katimanialuk* (Great Meeting) in Puvirnituq agreed to let things percolate for a while and convene again early in 1972 at Fort Chimo (Kuujjuaq). Lots of strong words had been exchanged, but nobody in either ideological camp became intractable enemies.

Founding the Northern Quebec
Inuit Association

Four months after the "rumble in the tundra" in Puvirnituq, Inuit leaders met again in January 1972 in Fort Chimo. This time, their mission was to decide the political future of Northern Quebec. I was then an employee of the federal government living in Great Whale River (Kuujjuaraapik). I don't remember how I "just happened to be there", but I was determined to be at this meeting. I wanted to witness history. This was the right place, at the right time, to be in!

This meeting was more focused, and discussions were not all over the map, as they had been at Puvirnituq four months earlier. Part of the dynamic was the emergence of natural leaders who seemed destined to also be in this right place, at this right time! Not many of the participants had any experience in contending with governments. But they more than made up for this deficit by being clear thinkers and articulate definers of their people's aspirations.

People's Hudson-vs-Ungava origins hit a few bumps, but were sorted out through instant familiarization with each other's ancestries and dialects. Aside from Co-op meetings, this meeting was the second in which Inuit themselves ran without supervision from government.

Eleven communities were represented; Umiujaq, Akulivik, and Aupaluk did not yet exist. Although the region's population was barely over 4,000, there was no sense of inferiority on that count.

People wanted Inuit to speak for themselves and assert their sense of place in the larger framework of the province and country they lived in. They were determined not to be mere pawns in the eternal federal-provincial tensions that never seemed to help Inuit in any way. Although the James Bay project was taking place almost exclusively in Cree country, Inuit wanted Inuit interests to be defended by Inuit, from an angle and source of Inuit strengths.

The Kuujjuaq meeting was marred by a tragedy in which three people died from drinking methyl alcohol. One of the people who died was a delegate, and the episode darkened the atmosphere. Charlie Watt, who was chairing the meeting, consulted elders and delegates about what to do. A clear consensus was made to not allow the tragedy to sideline the mission at hand – that of creating an entity called the Northern Quebec Inuit Association.

Charlie Watt was elected President of the new association. I was elected to its Board, three months short of my 21st birthday. We were ready to tackle the Great Unknown; it was a moment full of hope.

Leaders and Leadership

The collective life of Inuit in Northern Quebec was moved into overdrive by the invasion that was the James Bay project. It reached a milestone in January 1972. The Quebec government was allowing indiscriminate blasting and bulldozing of lands and rivers to build dams for hydroelectricity. The Cree people of James Bay and the Inuit of Northern Quebec actually had no choice but to stand up to the developers' and governments' "damn-all-opposition" arrogance.

The challenge was so monumental that some, Inuit as well as non-Inuit, questioned the logic of even taking it on. Some obvious concerns were raised: "How can a bunch of Eskimos contend with the government of Quebec and its all-powerful partners? Who can even contemplate wanting to stop one of the wonders of the universe – the James Bay project?" There was no shortage of nay-sayers. Uncommon resolve would be needed to rise to the occasion.

Fortunately, a group of Inuit took up the tasks of leadership, without in the least shrinking from the challenge. Prominent among these was Charlie Watt, a mechanic from Fort Chimo who was then living in George River. Charlie had an uncanny ability to sort through the trivial to get to the important stuff – the living embodiment of the "can-do" attitude. Another notable leader was Lazarusie Epoo from Port Harrison (Inukjuak), whose sharp intellect left no stone unturned for the Inuit cause.

Lazarusie's hard-charging energy contrasted with the serene and calm demeanor of Johnny Watt from Fort Chimo (Charlie's uncle). Johnny was a crystal-clear thinker – and a fortress of steadiness who never seemed to be perturbed by the roller-coaster turmoil of negative events happening in quick succession. Then there was Tommy Cain, a big man from Leaf Bay, the smallest community in the region, who was solid bedrock in human form.

Zebedee with Lazarusie Epoo from Port Harrison (Inukjuak). "[His] sharp intellect left no stone unturned for the Inuit cause."

(The names I'm so casually dropping here each deserve a chapter in their own right). Jacob Oweetaltuk of Port Harrison had been one of the first "general purpose" interpreters bridging the gap between Inuit and Qallunaat. I've often said that Jacob deserves a medal for almost single-handedly convincing the Inuit of Great Whale River to detach themselves from the Indians of Quebec Association and throw in their lot with the yet un-tested NQIA. I'd also have to write a separate chapter called, "The Humors of Jacob O".

These Inuit leaders conscientiously pioneered a path through totally unmarked political terrain. At first, they were little more than nagging nuisances to the titans of development, but in the end they threw a significant legal wrench into Quebec's tidy plans.

Inuit "Get in" Through Two Rivers

In April 1972, with the office of the new Northern Quebec Inuit Association still being set up, the James Bay Project was at the top of everybody's agenda. Yet, we had not acquired documented details of the project's global plans. Officialdom was not at all concerned about how Inuit in Northern Quebec might be affected by the Great Scheme to dam and divert river systems. But we immediately got busy searching for whatever facts we could find.

Somehow, Charlie Watt got his hands on a James Bay development map. It resembled a diagram for an epic fictional movie produced by a mastermind afflicted with full-blown "extreme colonialism on steroids". Quebec had created a principality called the Municipality of James Bay, 350,000 square kilometers in size, custommade to make approvals easier for the infrastructure of the project. There were no environmental review processes in those days.

When we examined these maps, we saw that two rivers in Inuit lands – the Great Whale and Caniapiscau – were to be partially dammed and diverted. The proponents of the project had *carte blanche* to do anything they wanted. There was no such thing as consulting or informing the Cree people, on whose lands this was being done.

Inuit were even worse off as inconsequential "outsiders" in the distant outer margins of Ground Zero.

In May 1972, we heard that Cree leaders from James Bay were meeting at Fort George, forerunner of today's town of Chisasibi. Charlie Watt and I immediately arranged to go there, to investigate what was going on. Inuit were not yet "players" in this whole business, but we were determined to cut through "long-distance curiosity" to define our stake in this whole thing. So without the least bit of hesitation, we walked into this meeting without being invited.

When we showed up at the meeting hall, we were questioned about the purpose of our presence. We plainly stated our mission: Two rivers in Inuit lands were part of the hydro scheme. Any efforts to seek compensation from Quebec and developers would have to include us Inuit. Once we said this, we were politely told to leave the room while Cree leaders and their advisors decided whether they would allow Inuit to be involved in their activities. At this time, Cree leaders had a lot on their plate. Their hunting and trapping grounds were literally being blasted to bits. But soon we were told that they had accepted our request to be included.

Shifting Political Outlooks

During their leaders' meeting in May 1972 in Fort George, the Cree of James Bay were processing and defining their capacities to speak for themselves, instead of having the Indians of Quebec Association speak for them. A group of younger "hands-on" doers were emerging among the Cree and influencing collective direction. Prominent among these was Chief Billy Diamond from Rupert House (Waskaganish), as well as others of his generation.

On our side, Inuit from Great Whale River had been members of IQA, and so had been attending Indian meetings. This overlapped with the Cree meeting in Fort George. The presence and support of a delegation of Inuit from Great Whale River (Kuujjuaraapik) at the Fort George meeting provided a favorable dynamic for Inuit inclusion in actions being mapped out. Brash as we had been in showing up uninvited, Charlie Watt and I were not the only advocates for Inuit participation.

Having to wrestle with the James Bay project was a pioneering activity for everybody. There were no other events comparable within anybody's memory that could serve as precedents for dealing with the twists and turns of this issue. Cree and Inuit were navigating through pathways never traveled before. But then, so were the developers and their government enablers. They hadn't expected the Cree and Inuit to take up being "idle no more" to complicate development plans. That night, we danced the jig with the best of them, and that seemed to seal the deal for a Cree-Inuit alliance to take on the developers of James Bay.

The Fort George meeting established the beginnings of a joint Cree-Inuit strategy to pursue something previously unthinkable: to take the government of Quebec and its development partners to court for violating the Aboriginal rights of the Cree of James Bay and the Inuit of Northern Quebec. This took some

Zebedee Nungak, Charlie Watt, and Josepi Padlayat. Charlie Watt was NQIA president and Inuit "team leader" during JBNQA negotiations. Josepi Padlayat, with George Koneak, was the Inuktitut interpreter for the James Bay court case.

courage and original thinking to formulate. We were familiar with David slaying Goliath in the Bible, but none of us even had an *illuuq* (sling) to attempt anything similar.

The political lay of the land was decidedly hostile to the Cree and Inuit. The only other force with any political muscle, which might have prevented Cree and Inuit from being totally crushed by the James Bay project, was the federal government. Our initial examinations of legal recourses found that the federal government had a "fiduciary responsibility" for Aboriginal people. But the government of Canada was not exactly rushing forth to protect Aboriginal people in James Bay and Northern Quebec from blatant exploitation. We would have to defend and protect, ourselves.

To Court! To Court!

Once the Cree and Inuit made the decision to seek a court injunction against the James Bay project, it took some double takes for the objective to sink in: We were going to court! *To court!* To stop the James Bay project! Whoever heard of Indians and Eskimos taking governments and big corporations to court? Yet we had crossed a threshold of no return and immediately got consumed in a frenzied, fantasy-cum-reality world which none of us had ever been in before!

We had to leave our homes, families, and normal lives, and become instant experts in suitcase/hotel/taxi/restaurant living. Furthermore, lawyers, courts, judges, witnesses, cross-examinations, and real legal mumbo-jumbo also had to be quickly mastered. The Cree seemed to be light-years ahead of us by having two lawyers in their employ since before the Fort George meeting. We had to instantly become as sophisticated as they were by finding lawyers.

My memories of the James Bay court case are a series of vivid but fragmented clips. The Cree had numerous elders who could describe every nook and cranny of the Municipality of James Bay, all 350,000 square kilometers of it! Cree elders conveyed intimate knowledge of the land that the government of Quebec had called "unorganized territory". They pointed to hunting and fishing grounds, trap-line boundaries, and ancestral burial sites.

We Inuit had three men who were authorities on Inuit land use. Tumasi Kudluk of Kangirsuk had been one of the last real *Nunamiut* (Inlanders) and was an expert on all aspects of the interior of what is now Nunavik. Elijah Angnatuk of Kuujjuaq had traveled vast distances in his lifetime, gaining an intimate knowledge of the land. Peter Iikkuluk Jonasie had worked for years with hydrographic surveys of the river systems which were now being developed.

Inuit spoke Inuktitut in court and needed interpreters. As one of the plaintiffs in the court action, I could not serve as an interpreter in the court proceedings. For this purpose, the court hired two extraordinarily competent Inuuk interpreters: George Aqiggiq Koneak and Josepi Padlayat. These two men performed superbly under the stress of having to make sense of super-legalese terminology.

Our adversaries in court were the best that money and power could supply: well-educated, experienced corporate heavyweights used to getting their way in matters big and small. They had been conducting "business as usual" when they were hauled into court by the Cree and Inuit. We contended with them on legalities, but also had to "educate" them.

"Educating" Corporations and Governments

The Montreal courthouse where the James Bay court case was being tried was not merely a court of law. It became also a schoolhouse-by-necessity where the scions of corporations and governments were taught lessons in elementary history, geography, and culture by the Cree and Inuit. It was an amazing revelation to find that "well-educated" people were so unlearned about the existence of Aboriginal people in this part of the country. We had to teach them!

The first lesson was that the territory being invaded wholesale by the James Bay project actually had people living in it. This was somewhat shocking to people who regarded James Bay and Northern Quebec as virgin territory ripe for the taking, notwithstanding any bothersome people getting in the way of their Grand Scheme. We had to cite archeological studies, which had carbon-dated over 4,000 years of continuous occupation of the land we were fighting for.

The extension of this lesson was that we lived "off the land". We subsisted on all manner of wildlife, which sustained us right to the present day: fish, caribou, migratory birds, plants and berries, as well as marine mammals in the case of Inuit. The developers and governments we hauled into court found it highly inconvenient to be told that the land that was being blasted and bulldozed was a life-giving environment to the people who had lived there from time immemorial.

Cree and Inuit had been stewards and caretakers of their environment for millennia. The proposed diversion of rivers and creation of gigantic man-made reservoirs were sure to result in irreversible damage to the ecology, flora, and fauna of the Cree and Inuit homeland. We freely expressed heartfelt concern about how the destruction of vast ecosystems was going to affect our future generations.

The only thing the government and their corporate henchmen were certain about was that the government of Canada had transferred jurisdiction over these lands north of the Eastmain River to Quebec in 1898, and again in 1912 to the high water mark of the Hudson Bay, Hudson Strait and Ungava Bay coasts. As far as they were concerned, they had every right to do as they wanted on these lands. We had to pointedly remind them that we had never been conquered in war by any outsiders. Neither had we ever signed any treaties or established formal relationships with whoever was presuming to "govern" our lands. We found the courtroom to be a perfect classroom to teach concepts foreign to the mindsets of governments and corporations.

Colonialism on Steroids vs. Assertive Aboriginality

The James Bay court case is formally identified as Kanatewat et al v. James Bay Development Corp. et al. The name is derived from Robert Kanatewat, at the time Chief of Fort George, forerunner of the town of Chisasibi, and one of the signatories of the James Bay Agreement. This name is forever attached to a Quebec Superior Court decision, which triggered negotiations between the Aboriginal people and governments/developers.

The Aboriginal rationale for this case was based on the following logic: "Our Aboriginal rights have been violated by the project. Nobody consulted or notified us before our lands were blasted for dams and diversion of rivers. Our rights exist, not merely because we say so, but because laws made in Canada specifically mention them in identifiable legislation without enumerating their contents. Unlawful acts are being committed against us through this Project!"

For references we pointed to section 91 (24) of the British North America Act and the Quebec Boundaries Extension Acts of 1898 and 1912. We could also cite the Supreme Court of Canada 1939 decision. Quebec had taken the federal government to court in 1936, pleading that it had no legal obligations toward Eskimos in the lands it acquired in 1912, and won!

Governments and developers followed their own narrow logic: "We have the consent and approval of the Quebec government, which has jurisdiction over these lands. We are within our legal capacities to do this work, for the economic benefit of all Quebecers." The case could be given an alternative title, that captures the essence of two forces, which collided head-on in a Montreal courtroom: "Colonialism on Steroids v. Assertive Aboriginality".

The following questions should be raised: Why do developers disregard the Cree and Inuit dependency for life itself on the land, rivers, and sea? How does the Quebec government treat governmental legal obligations toward Cree and Inuit? Governments and developers had acted as if Aboriginal rights didn't exist, or were of no importance. Now Aboriginal people were using the legal system to ascertain and defend their rights.

Prior to the James Bay project, settler governments had used colonial and post-colonial legalities of European origin to assign to Aboriginal lands whatever jurisdictional status pleased them. They had initially launched the project in the way they had always done business. But this time it was different; a Cree-Inuit alliance was directly inserting Aboriginal interests and realities into a process that had long enjoyed unobstructed freedom to do as it pleased.

The Essence of the Malouf Decision

It's been more than forty years since the Inuit and Cree teamed up in court to oppose the James Bay project. My recollection of that legal battle has become increasingly fallible. This is an excerpt from a description found on the Grand Council of the Crees website entitled Role of the Canadian Courts in Aboriginal Rights:

> ...the Crees and Inuit of Northern Quebec in 1972 went to Court seeking an injunction to halt work (that had already begun) on the James Bay hydro-electric project. The resultant Court case was a landmark in Canadian legal history. The Quebec government lawyers went into Court arguing that they had no case to answer, that Aboriginal rights had never existed in the province, and so far as they had been mentioned in other parts of Canada were too vaguely defined to have any meaning.
>
> Quebec Superior Court Justice Albert Malouf, however, decided that there was a case to answer, and spent almost six months hearing evidence from Cree and Inuit hunters about their relationship with, attitude towards, and contemp-

orary use of, the land. The case was the first in Canadian history in which a cohesive group of people, in this case Cree and Inuit hunters, argued that the integrity of the environment was essential to their survival as peoples.

Justice Malouf found in favor of the Cree and Inuit. He ordered work on the project to be stopped, and Quebec to cease trespassing on Cree and Inuit lands. His judgment was overturned quickly by the Quebec Appeal Court, but the Malouf judgment had such weight that it forced the Quebec and Canadian governments to negotiate a treaty (...the James Bay and Northern Quebec Agreement) which was signed in 1975.

To return to the biblical analogy of David and Goliath, the Cree and Inuit had used the Quebec Superior Court as a sling, and brought Premier Bourassa's Project of the Century to a screeching halt. Justice Malouf's decision was the smooth stone in the sling that hit the James Bay project Goliath on its head with enough force to temporarily "kill" it for one week. Construction was halted. Our work in court had not gone unrewarded.

Negotiate! Negotiate!

The victory handed down to us by Justice Albert Malouf was a stunning achievement. But we didn't have any time to celebrate. We had hardly squared our shoulders to appreciate the win when we heard that our adversaries, Hydro-Québec and the government, were immediately appealing the decision to the Quebec Court of Appeals. Right away, we were at risk of losing everything, without any chance to assess just what we had gained.

The Malouf decision caused the machinery and construction of the James Bay project to stop in its tracks. Furthermore, Justice Malouf ordered Quebec and its development agents to "cease trespassing on Cree and Inuit lands". Having the court tell that to Quebec was a wonderful, natural, high. Fleeting as this victory was, it gave Cree and Inuit leaders an invigorating shot of self-confidence. For one brief shining moment, fate had dealt us a good hand.

Then, the Court of Appeals overturned Justice Malouf's injunction, and work resumed within a week. This was based on something called the "balance of convenience", meaning the interests of a few (Cree and Inuit) could not supersede the interests of the many (the general populace of Quebec). Construction resumed, but, crucially, our Aboriginal rights remained, as established by Justice Malouf.

The Goliath we had struck had lain motionless on the ground for one week. When Justice Malouf's injunction was overturned, we faced a burdensome decision: Should we go to the Supreme Court of Canada hoping to have the reversal overturned? Should we risk all or nothing? In the Bible, David didn't have to deal with Goliath coming back to life again. There were no more examples to draw upon for inspiration.

In allowing developers to begin destroying James Bay territory, Quebec had totally neglected any regard for Aboriginal rights, and ignored legal obligations toward the territory's Aboriginal people spelled out in the Boundaries Extension Acts of 1898 and 1912. Quebec was not at all enlightened about the concept of Aboriginal people having rights. In this context, it was difficult to imagine having to negotiate anything with them. As well, the federal government, which held fiduciary responsibility for Aboriginal people, was equally dumbfounded about what to do next.

Processing all of this was surreal, like being inside a science fiction production, yet somehow, it was all rock-hard reality. There were no how-to manuals to guide us, and no soothing doctrine available to help us avoid mistakes which could result in irreparable damage to our mission. Here, we relied solely on Ancient Aboriginal instinct. As we seemed to spin involuntarily in the aftermath of the court case, a clear directive issued to all parties suddenly came down: Negotiate! Negotiate!

Negotiations, Cold Turkey

So far, I've written nearly 7,000 words just to sum up the background of how Inuit got involved in the court case against the James Bay project. I'm now somewhat intimidated by having to share some of my recollections of the negotiations that followed. I cannot provide a clinical chronology of everything that unfolded because I wasn't at every table. A complete historical account will have to involve all the surviving Inuit veterans.

In July 2010, I was invited to be one of the panelists at the Qanak Youth Conference in Inukjuak, to talk about the James Bay experience. The other panelists were Charlie Watt, Sarollie Weetaluktuk, and Lazarusie Epoo. After the panelists spoke, the forum was opened to delegates for a freewheeling question-and-answer session. Many raw emotions surfaced in the exchanges. Even the panelists choked up as we released some pent-up emotions with our recollections.

The story of the negotiations for the James Bay Agreement is overflowing with all sorts of heavy baggage, some of it raw garbage. The whole process is loaded with contradictions and paradoxes. It's a "success story" that also contains abject failures. In the mix are profound losses and tiny victories, intense duress, impossible deadlines, and unsavory compromises, having to deal with overt "civilized" evil and deeply divisive Inuit-on-Inuit confrontations.

As I stated near the beginning of this story, the James Bay negotiations were not triggered by the parties saying, "Let's negotiate the James Bay Agreement!" during a friendly Saturday afternoon visit. Negotiating with the Cree and Inuit was never in the original plans of the government of Quebec and its development partners. But a court ordered Quebec to "cease trespassing on Cree and Inuit lands." For a jurisdiction that was confident of its "boss-hood" over the lands in question since 1898 and 1912, being told to stop trespassing on somebody else's land had to sting. Being forced to deal with Aboriginals produced an underlying resentment, which was never far from the surface throughout the negotiations.

Established powers can hold deep grudges, and there's never any shortage of these in Quebec at any time. None of us had any on-the-job-training, or seminars, to ease us into a sense of what the other parties in upcoming negotiations were all about, and where each was coming from. All of us entered into negotiations cold turkey.

Opposing Lines: Youth vs. Establishment

It's worth reviewing the opposing lines that were involved in the negotiations that produced the James Bay and Northern Quebec Agreement. Remember, the Aboriginal parties had skipped and skimmed through a dizzying series of statuses in a very short time. They were first utterly insignificant as the Project of the Century was announced. Then, they were unavoidable legal nuisances during the court case. Now, they were *bona fide* parties that had to be negotiated with!

This could be compared to "ordinary peasants" becoming grudgingly tolerated in the boardrooms of the rich and powerful who aren't known to be disposed toward talks with such people. The negotiations were forced upon them, triggering a dialogue with people they would otherwise have nothing to do with. The so-called playing field here was greatly lopsided – developers and governments were obsessed with getting on with their project.

Cree and Inuit leaders were equally determined to attain real gains for their people, however impossible such a task appeared to be. There were no more than around sixty people combined working for the Cree and Inuit during the two years of negotiations. I heard that about three hundred support workers and bureaucrats backed up the governments and developers. I've never doubted that estimate, which illustrates how greatly outnumbered we were.

What the Cree and Inuit lacked in numbers, they made up for in exuberant youthful energy. Most of our frontline workers were very young and nonchalant about the impossibilities they encountered almost daily. Many of us were barely past our first shave – in the archival footage and photographs we look like kids. By contrast, those who represented governments and developers were mostly 50- or 60-somethings, brimming with piles of formal education, establishment pedigree, corporate oomph and doo-dah, and plenty of formidable governmental know-how.

Mark R. Gordon was the chief negotiator for the Inuit. He got into the job fresh out of art school, where he had almost forgotten how to speak Inuktitut. He immediately became an effective, competent force to be reckoned with by our adversaries, and regained fluency in Inuktitut almost overnight. It was awesome to observe Mark blossom into a professional marvel of a man. All Inuit who contributed to our effort should be recognized. History had them, maybe not in the right place at the right time, but neither were they in the wrong place at the wrong time.

Opposing Parameters

The first face-to-face sessions at the negotiating table were extremely awkward. To each other, we were like aliens from different worlds. Our respective jigsaw puzzle pieces didn't come close to fitting together at all. The circumstances under which we met weren't conducive to leisurely, stress-free diplomacy. We tried not to act like mortal enemies, but it was impossible to be buddy-buddy. It didn't help that we all, on both sides, spoke in a second language, English.

On the matter of land, our position was: "We've never been conquered in war; we've never signed a treaty. We own every inch of our traditional lands. We may permit certain developments, if our people can attain tangible benefits." Quebec's attitude was: "In the *status* of our *quo*, we are the Bosses; we have legal authority over all land. You need our permission to attain any benefits from this land, over which we are *maîtres chez nous*."

On rights, our position was: "We certainly have rights, the source of which spring from our occupation of this land from time immemorial." Quebec's attitude was: "We cannot acknowledge the existence of 'rights' that are not defined and/or catalogued as to their content and extent." We reminded Quebec that a court of theirs had ordered them to "cease trespassing on Cree and Inuit lands."

On self-government, our position was: "We need a government that will assure autonomous self-determination for our people/territory." Quebec's attitude was: "In this country, there's the federal government, the provincial/territorial governments, and municipal governments. There's no such thing as Aboriginal Government." I remember Quebec representatives actually laughing in derisive mockery at our first presentations on this subject.

One anomaly of the negotiations was the presence of officials from hydro, energy, and development corporations at the table. Not knowing of other negotiations we could emulate, we didn't make a big deal of having the blasters and dynamiters at the table to directly protect and promote their interests. The only development interests missing at the negotiations table were owners of scores of mining and mineral claims, which dotted the map of what is now Nunavik. But they were absent in name only. Quebec was ruthlessly determined not to allow known mineral claims to become owned by the Inuit. Their attitude was, "natural wealth belongs to everybody – not just you!" Quebec had gained jurisdictional authority over the land by colonial osmosis and had overseen mineral claims registered in the territory since the 1950s. Overt greed backed up by raw power was part of Quebec's approach to negotiations.

The Basics Become Apparent

The Northern Quebec Inuit Association represented its members through a legal instrument called power of attorney. This was a document signed by members to give their consent to the Association to negotiate on their behalf with the government of Quebec, the government of Canada, and the development corporations. NQIA's mandate was based on these signatures. These powers of attorney would figure prominently when some members withdrew them later on.

The NQIA was given a very serious responsibility by its members; no such trust had ever been given or held before. For the first time in history, Inuit were sitting directly at a table with various jurisdictions and principalities to define formal relationships, which had never been considered in 1670, 1867, 1898, and 1912. We were to crash head-on into the consequences of colonial acts from those years, in which our ancestral lands were treated as real estate playthings.

As negotiations bored through a tunnel of various practical and political impossibilities, certain basic elements of any future agreement began to emerge. These issues became unavoidable as Quebec hardened its positions. The most difficult of these metamorphosed into take-it-or-leave-it issues, as Quebec edged close to impatient nastiness on these matters.

First, there was to be an "extinguishment and surrender" clause, which the Cree and Inuit were expected to agree to in exchange for rights and benefits enumerated in the agreement. This was alluded to in the 1912 Quebec Boundaries Extension Act. Governments wanted finality in their first settling of formal relationships with the Cree and Inuit. It was a concept utterly foreign to us.

Second, land to be held in ownership by the Inuit was to be a tiny fraction of the total land surface of the territory. This was very hard to swallow. I had not yet seen Bantustans, black "homelands" on the map of Apartheid South Africa. Original people's lands, it seemed, became the property of Qallunaat by divine default. Category-1 land, to be "owned" by Inuit were minuscule in size; yet Quebec considered itself too generous in even agreeing to them.

Third, there was to be no autonomous or semi-independent "government" for the territory. What was discussed was a "regional municipality", which Quebec resisted tooth and nail all the way, even insisting that it be called merely an *administration régionale*. The thought of Inuit becoming too independent was anathema to Quebec.

Working against stiff resistance doubled with gross heavy-handedness was sometimes disheartening. But it also sharpened our operating skills.

We Fire Our Lawyers

Some days were just wild and surreal. One of these was the day we fired our lawyers, right in the heat of negotiations. It went like this. Lawyers working for certain other negotiating parties had extracted financial commitments from their clients and would be paid sizable monetary bonuses upon a final agreement being achieved. When word of this got around, the two lawyers working for the Inuit decided to pursue similar benefits for themselves.

As soon as their request landed on the desk of our president, an emergency NQIA Board of Directors' meeting was convened to discuss the matter. The Board met in the NQIA's president's corner office on the 15th floor of 555 Dorchester Boulevard in Montreal. At the height of the discussion, in barged one of the bonus-seeking lawyers, on urgent other business. Panic was not an option.

Fortunately, I was in the midst of translating the substance of the issue in Inuktitut. There and then I discovered my professional acting skills when I instantly changed the subject of discussion. We started talking about everything except the lawyers. The other people in the room demonstrated their own superb acting skills when they got deeply into other subjects on cue. Everybody played his and her part perfectly in an Academy Award performance.

The lawyer left the room, not in the least suspecting that his Inuit clients were deciding his fate and that of his colleague. Our decision was to firmly refuse our lawyers' request for monetary bonuses. Our negotiations were being financed through borrowed money, repayable upon an agreement being concluded, which was not at all a sure thing. We ourselves were barely making expenses. It wasn't hard to say *no* to this proposition. We weren't in this to make certain people rich!

Our principle was: Nobody, including "indispensable" lawyers, would get any bonuses. We fired them that very afternoon, and our president went forth to search for other lawyers without skipping a beat. He very quickly found another law firm. We met our new lawyers, told them of our hard-work-but-no-bonus policy, briefed them on the latest issues at hand, and returned to our previously intense rhythms of work, work, work!

Of course, this could have crippled our efforts at a very crucial time. Lawyers' advice and input seemed to be the lifeblood of what was being constructed. But by then, many of us had also developed our own reasonably competent legal minds. I myself could even translate *ipso facto* and *mutatis mutandis* into Inuktitut!

Making Impossibilities Possible

Subjects other than the main important issues required our undivided attention at certain times. Some of these had first been discussed with the Cree, who were treated as the primary Aboriginal party by government and developers. Inuit, regarded as a secondary party, came upon such items in a more roundabout way. One such example was the Hunter's Support Program.

Quebec had tabled a proposition for a hunters' support program, and had seriously discussed the issue with the Cree. When the proposed program was first presented to us, we didn't want to talk much about it at all. I stand to be corrected by my fellow veterans on this, but I recall that we felt that hunting ought not to be turned into a program involving monetary gain. Sharing the harvest of hunts freely was a basic foundation of Inuit traditions, and we didn't want to commercialize this activity.

We were quite indifferent to Quebec's efforts to convince us to accept the program. We treated it as an attempted enticement to get us to be more accepting of the other problematic unattractive parts of the agreement that was being put together. Devising a hunters' assistance regime was not very high on our scheme of priorities. So, the Inuit Hunters' Support program ended up being less lucrative than the Cree regime, which the Cree more diligently negotiated.

Another issue vigorously promoted by Quebec was a provision allowing Qallunaat to become beneficiaries of the agreement through marriage. Here, Quebec decided to act as the champion of Qallunaat being entitled to Inuit rights. Inuit vehemently objected to this. How on earth can White people be turned into Eskimos? None of us had ever known Qallunaat in the Arctic as downtrodden, second-class citizens needing special rights. The primary purpose of our negotiations was to establish Inuit rights, not enhance the already bountiful well-being of Qallunaat! This issue generated a number of choice words and vividly colorful language among the Inuit negotiators. Qallunaat having the same rights as Inuit to hunt and fish sounded like a fable from Fantasyland. We didn't have any problem accepting non-Inuit as normal members of our communities through marriage. But granting them rights attained through great tribulation didn't sit well with us at all. Our genuine rational objections counted for nothing since Quebec simply rammed through the impossibility of Whites becoming legally regarded as Eskimos, in the name of "family cohesion". Nothing was impossible, if Quebec wanted it.

Public Services, Non-Ethnic Institutions

Here, I'll deliberately fast-forward to discuss public services and non-ethnic institutions. Whole sections of the James Bay Agreement seem out of place in an exclusively Aboriginal land claims agreement. These sections deal with provision of normal, regular services that governments provide to their citizens without them being required to beg for such services.

Here's a list of public services provided in the JBN-QA: Local Government North of the 55th parallel (Section 12); Regional Government North of the 55th parallel (Section 13); Health and Social Services – Inuit (Section 15); Education – Inuit (Section 17); Administration of Justice – Inuit (Section 20); Police – Inuit (Section 21); Environment and Future Development North of the 55th parallel (Section 23); Inuit Social and Economic Development (Section 29).

One might think, "Wow! We gained a lot: health, education, municipal, environment, administration of justice, economic development!" But here's the catch: Nobody else in Quebec ever had to trade the essence of their identity to gain access to public services. New immigrants and their descendants were entitled to these without having to make extraordinary, cataclysmic concessions in exchange.

These services should have been delivered without any fuss to the people of Nunavik, starting from ship time in the summer of 1912, after our land was transferred to Quebec in April of that year. But nothing happened until the summer of 1964, when René Lévesque, then Minister of Natural Resources in Liberal Premier Jean Lesage's government, came to Fort Chimo (Kuujjuaq), to declare Quebec's intention to be present in what it called Nouveau-Québec. Quebec's sudden discovery of its northern territory was simply too abrupt for some Inuit leaders to absorb. Lévesque's presentation resounded with patronization: "Know ye this, we're now the Bosses around here".

Jacob Oweetaltuk, an outspoken young man at that meeting, asked Mr. Lévesque: "In all those years, when you were knowingly the government of this land, why didn't you erect an outpost, even the size of an outhouse, somewhere here?"

Quebec's services deficit was more than sixty years of not providing any to Inuit citizens in Nunavik. Now, it was presenting its services for the first time as part of an ethnic land claims deal. How enormously generous! Or so we were supposed to think. But, we were simply too busy trying to tie down our Aboriginal rights to pointedly dwell on Quebec's extreme tardiness on its public service obligations.

No Clean, Pre-Colonial Slate

At one of the Aboriginal Constitutional First Ministers Conferences in the 1980s, First Nations Chief James Gosnell from British Columbia stood up and declared, "We own this land: lock, stock, and barrel, from the North Pole to the tip of South America!" In reply, Prime Minster Pierre Trudeau arrogantly asked this rhetorical question, "I mean, from where do you want to start? Creation?" I've always regretted not saying, "No, Prime Minister! Let's start from May 2, 1670!"

Now, back to the James Bay negotiations: The trials and tribulations experienced by the Inuit of Nunavik in those negotiations have their roots in colonial history. Negotiations were not conducted on a clean, pre-colonial slate. The starting clock could not be set back to the day before a colonial act by a foreign king colored our ancestral lands British red for all time on that day in 1670. When the James Bay project was launched, neither Quebec nor Ottawa had bothered to check the fine print of the last land transfer they had enacted in 1912. When the Quebec government barreled ahead with the project, the federal government didn't grab it by the shoulder and say, "Wait a minute, deal first with Aboriginal rights!"

It had been post-colonial business as usual until the Cree and Inuit took the legal steps that eventually triggered the start of negotiations. The federal and provincial governments had been very generous to each other in the years they enacted land transfers with total abandon. No Aboriginal groups interfered with their land acts in 1898 and 1912. There were no hearings, consultations, or informing notice of these acts to people who had always lived on these lands.

The federal government held responsibility for "Indians and lands reserved for Indians" under section 91 (24) of the British North America Act, since 1867. This didn't prevent it from simply giving away vast tracts of Aboriginal territory to provinces, which were very eager recipients of such largesse. When the Cree of James Bay and Inuit of Nunavik finally sat down with governments in 1974, these governments held absolute power over all lands in question. They felt legally and constitutionally self-enabled to extract extreme concessions from the Cree and Inuit. This they did by requiring them to "extinguish and surrender Aboriginal title in and to (the) land" in dispute.

Agreement-in-Principle, 1974

There was never a laid-back, take-it-easy lull during negotiations. Quebec and its development partners were possessed by a self-impelling frenzy, which permeated the atmosphere of negotiations. The pulse of it was, "Rush, Rush, RUSH!" The rumble and clatter of earth-moving machinery and blasting in James Bay was practically audible in the boardrooms of Montreal where negotiations were taking place. It was Go! Go! Go! – all the way.

Eventually, intense negotiations forged the basic elements of a possible agreement. Its terms included: i) Extinguishment and surrender of Aboriginal title in and to the lands in question. ii) Measured areas of land, to be held in ownership by Inuit, designated Category-1 lands. iii) A "regional municipality"; not the legislation producing "government" which Inuit had pursued in negotiations against determined resistance from Quebec.

On November 15, 1974, exactly one year after Judge Malouf's verdict, an Agreement-in-Principle (AIP) was signed. It detailed these things, along with an elementary list of rights to be recognized. In that time, the Great Rush had transformed negotiations into a creature from which all negotiating parties couldn't simply walk away. Veterans of the experience will have to air the layered reasons for not simply refusing to sign the document. There existed no examples set by other groups for us to follow to do this right. Attempting to produce a rights-defining, life-altering document in the vise-grip of a process driven by the imperatives of development interests backed overtly by government complicity and support was incredibly difficult.

Inuit working for the NQIA took the document to all the eleven communities to explain its contents to the people. The process was not to ask what people wanted changed or improved in the deal. It was, instead, "Here is the framework of the deal offered, without much prospect of increase by the governments and the development corporations."

A sizable segment of the Inuit population said *no* to the contents of the AIP: They objected to extinguishment and surrender of rights, and they considered the land that would be owned by Inuit to be insultingly tiny. They were also very unhappy with the lack of a stand-alone government for the territory. Dissidents asserted that any gains made in exchange for these extreme concessions were not worth it. They felt betrayed by the NQIA leadership, and forthrightly said so. The world as we knew it erupted into turmoil and disagreement, the likes of which Inuit had never known.

Inuuqatigiit Tunngavingat Nunamini (ITN)

The Agreement-in-Principle reached in November 1974 was not accepted by everybody. Inuit in Puvirnituq, Ivujivik, and part of Salluit disagreed so profoundly with what had been negotiated that they withdrew their powers-of-attorney from the NQIA. At first, they were called *Naammasanngituit* in Inuktitut – dissidents in English. As their opposition to the AIP became more widely known, they took the name *Inuuqatigiit Tunngavingat Nunamini*, or ITN.

ITN was not a legally registered corporate entity. It was a coalition of individuals who took a name for the cause of expressing opposition to the James Bay Agreement. They later changed the first word of their name, *Inuuqatigiit*, to simply *Inuit*, to make the name less of a mouthful for the stiff tongues of non-Inuit who were interested in the activities and ideology of ITN.

ITN's outspoken leaders' position was that Inuit were still complete and absolute masters of their unceded ancestral lands. The Inuit negotiators, accused by ITN of giving in to such conditions, were called sell-outs. People entrenched themselves into pro- and anti-agreement factions. Heated arguments degenerated into personal attacks and even hateful exchanges. People talked *at* each other, and not *to* each other. Harmony among families and friends was violated in ways that had never happened before among Inuit.

ITN's opposition to the James Bay Agreement gained traction even outside its base of two and a half communities in Nunavik. Prominent Inuit spokespeople from other regions of Arctic Canada expressed support for ITN's positions. I recall hearing leaders from what is now Nunavut saying, "We will never agree to the extinguishment and surrender of our Aboriginal rights!" They claimed they would do better than us on that point, and I'd think, "All power to you on that!"

ITN used every available means at their disposal to try to stop the James Bay Agreement. They went to

Public meeting in Puvirnituq. Standing at the microphone is Eliassie Sallualuk, one of the leaders and spokesmen for the Inuuqatigiit Tunngavingat Nunamini (ITN), which opposed the James Bay Agreement.

parliamentary hearings in Ottawa and Quebec City to proclaim their opposition. They conducted a widespread publicity campaign. They took legal action against the parties that had negotiated the agreement. None of this succeeded in stopping the juggernaut of the JBNQA. The political system proved to be highly resistant to sustained, principled opposition.

To this day, ITN has an active court case against the JBNQA on file. This case has not been dismissed, and its merits need to be proved or disproved. The great contentions and turmoil Inuit went through for this should not be for nothing. And the ITN story has to be told by those who promoted its objectives.

Analyzing Extinguishment & Surrender

To the Inuit who opposed the terms of the proposed agreement, the clause defining "extinguishment and surrender of Aboriginal title in and to land" was a blatant sell-out. The Inuit negotiators who had agreed to this clause were criticized, derided, mocked, belittled, and even hated. Who in his and her right mind would agree to such debasement? Weren't we Inuit always the owners of our vast ancestral lands? Where did this despicable surrender come from?

Inuit occupation of the Arctic, confirmed by archeologists, has been dated at 4,000 years. Here we were facing descendants of immigrants who had been here for only 365 years. But these recent arrivals held a lock on all the land. Their imported system of governing was based on absolute, structural superiority over lands and peoples their forbears had "discovered."

Indians or Eskimos had never participated in European immigrants' law-making institutions where "extinguishment and surrender of Aboriginal title in and to lands" was invented and preserved for future usage. Not a thought was ever given to consulting or even informing the Aboriginal inhabitants of these lands, as their lands were carved up and allocated willy-nilly among governing units who held dictatorial powers over all they surveyed, and then some.

More leisurely negotiations with more time to unhurriedly argue the fine points of the most important issues may not have altered the outcome, or have the extinguishment and surrender clause replaced with something less draconian. Here's why: The James Bay negotiations took two years – a rush job if ever there was one. The 1984 Inuvialuit Final Agreement in the Western Arctic took eight years to negotiate. Nunavut Land Claims Agreement (1993) took 17 years, and Labrador (Nunatsiavut) Inuit Land Claims Agreement (2005) took 27 years – yet none of these land claims agreements escaped the black mark of "extinguishment and surrender" in exchange for rights and benefits. Governments of the land in Canada insisted on this measure as a mandatory basis for settling original peoples' claims, on a "once-and-for-all" basis.

For the sin of being the first Inuit group to be threaded through the needle of extinguishment and surrender, we took the brunt of the body blows of ridicule, and worse. Inuit in other Arctic regions who were later forced across this threshold by governments didn't get so much as a mild scolding from their people. This is one stretch of trailblazing that I would've preferred to leave for others to pioneer. But it fell on our lot, and hurt us mightily.

Analyzing Inuit-Owned Lands

In a just and fair world, original inhabitants of Inuit lands ought to have been the acknowledged holders of all the land their ancestors had wandered for millennia. Inuit had never knowingly ceded their land to others, or lost it in war. Immigrants from other lands should have required permission from the land's original occupants about what they could do and where they could do it. But history had somehow twisted this equation, and turned it totally upside down.

The negotiations became the venue of this brutal discovery: immigrants held all the land while original inhabitants held nothing! Somewhere in the timeline, Qallunaat had become Boss of all the land. Occupation of the land from time immemorial was not a defining factor for original peoples' legal and constitutional currency in the imported European legal-political system.

Even now, it's difficult to wrap one's mind around the paradox of Inuit being forced to claim what they believed had been their own lands *from the Qallunaat*. Imagine the English having to claim Trafalgar Square in London from Inuit who claim to own it after they "discovered" it. Imagine the French having to claim the Eiffel Tower from a bunch of Eskimos who simply took it over one day. It sounds absurd. But when Qallunaat did such things, it was considered entirely normal.

Critics of the Agreement had much to be critical about the Category-1 lands to be owned by Inuit. They derisively called these lands *sikkitaapiit* (tiny squares). Not only were they tiny in size compared to the total expanse of the territory; Inuit would only own the surface rights, and not the subsurface. Quebec went to great pains to prevent any known mineral or other wealth from being owned by Inuit.

Land selection was the toughest item to settle. Inuit negotiators were caught between the "rock" of dissidents' mockery and the "hard place" of Quebec considering itself too generous already, giving Inuit too much land. In marathon sessions, Inuit elders marking maps to select land almost came to blows many times with Quebec negotiators, who went as far as grabbing the wrists of Inuit to prevent them from selecting certain areas. For example, Quebec insisted that registered mineral claims in the minerals-rich Ungava Trough be out of bounds for Inuit claims. Inuit-owned lands were further degraded by certain areas selected across bays and rivers being designated "Category-1 Special", to provide easier access to them by non-Inuit. Claiming bits of our ancestral land from Qallunaat filled us with negative karma.

Attaining Regional Municipality,
Not "Government"

When we Inuit in Nunavik first talked of wanting a "government" for our territory in the early 1970s, it was based on the desire to be able to make laws for ourselves, our land, and our lives. Being ruled from Ottawa and Quebec City had held no advantage for our identity, language, and culture. In the James Bay negotiations, we aimed to attain a "government" but only managed to get a "regional municipality". To many Inuit, this was not their idea of government.

In 1974, it was the height of fearless boldness for any Aboriginal group to actively seek formal, government-sanctioned ways and means to self-determination. Representing 4,000 people living in a region larger than California, we were the very embodiment of such fearless boldness. We challenged the government of Quebec to be innovative.

Serious discussion of the concept of the "Aboriginal right to self-government" in Canadian politics was more than a decade away, in the First Ministers Conferences of the 1980s. Nunavut was not yet a serious dream. When Inuit inserted this subject into the James Bay negotiations, governments were severely bent out of shape, but this didn't prevent us from going for it.

When the concept of an autonomous government for Northern Quebec was presented, Quebec gave us a stern lecture on how governments worked in the *status quo*. There was the federal government. There were the provincial and territorial governments. Then there were municipal or local governments. There was no space for any other form or level of government; least of all "Aboriginal" government, which was unheard of, and "simply impossible".

Federal and provincial jurisdictions had always found ways to carve up North America into "governed" units on the whim and fancy of immigrants who considered themselves superior to original peoples. When surveying straight lines for boundaries was inconvenient, their rulers turned vividly descriptive: "All lands flowing into Hudson Bay" (Rupert's Land, 1670), "Up to the high water mark" (Quebec expansion, 1912). Nothing was too hard to fix.

Even in 1974, it was "too hard" for the Quebec government to agree to a "government" for Northern Quebec. Negotiations finally distilled the subject down to a stark choice: a non-ethnic regional municipality covering the territory north of the 55th parallel or, alternatively, an Inuit-only government applicable only on Inuit-owned lands. Wanting influence over the whole territory, not just Inuit-owned lands, Inuit opted for the regional municipality. This was not the "stand-alone" government we had wanted, but it was better than nothing.

New Communities and Killinirmiut Inclusion

At the start of James Bay negotiations, only eleven Inuit villages existed in Northern Quebec. Negotiations coincided with some Inuit groups seeking to resettle in areas where they had lived prior to establishment of settlements. One of these was at Akulivik, near Cape Smith on the Hudson coast. Another was at Aupaluk, in Hopes Advance Bay on the Ungava coast. These two places attained official recognition as *bona fide* municipalities through the James Bay Agreement.

Inuit who worked to establish Akulivik and Aupaluk had always longed to return to their former surroundings. Prior to negotiations, they had struggled to re-establish a life in these locations, living in self-made shacks. In normal circumstances, the federal and provincial governments were extremely reluctant to accommodate the establishment of new northern communities: Services and infrastructure for such places didn't come cheap for cost-conscious governments.

Another prospective community's future was mapped out through the Agreement. The Inuit of Kuujjuaraapik had to confront the real possibility of their community being radically uprooted by future development of the Great Whale River. Weighing these probabilities caused them to select ownership lands in the Richmond Gulf area. A provision for a future vote to determine the question of forming a possible community in that area was written-in. Such a vote was carried out in the years following the Agreement and resulted in the establishment of the municipality of Umiujaq in 1986. The approvals for these three new communities in the region were major accomplishments and increased the number of Nunavik communities to fourteen.

Another major issue resolved was the inclusion of the Inuit of Port Burwell (Killiniq) in the negotiated land regime. The community of Killiniq was in the Northwest Territories, and thus in the jurisdiction of the NWT. Although the area was blessed with abundant wildlife resources, Killiniq's viability as a community had become an overwhelming burden for the NWT territorial government.

Here was one instance of a government being "too poor" to provide infrastructure such as an airstrip, and services such as health care to its citizens. Eventually, the community of Port Burwell was abandoned by the GNWT. Its residents were scattered in various communities on the Ungava coast as "refugees" living in communities, which were not assisted in any way by governments to provide basic necessities for these people.

But not everything in the Agreement was beyond redemption. Good things also resulted from it. The people living in these communities can thank the JBNQA for that.

Heavy-Handed Threat & Federal Weakness

Inuit in Puvirnituq (near the mouth of the Povungnituk River on Hudson Bay), and the northernmost community of Ivujivik refused to have anything to do with the James Bay Agreement. In a third community, Salluit, close to the Hudson Strait, slightly more than half of the people were dissidents. But the remainder of its population supported the agreement and fully participated in its related activities. Although the community was torn by divided loyalties, representatives from Salluit adhering to NQIA took part in the land selection process and selected Category-1 lands.

However, people in Puvirnituq and Ivujivik absolutely refused to mark any lands on the map. This should have been clearly understood, and the two communities left blank on the map. But Quebec did two arbitrary things: First, a 25-mile radius from the Puvirnituq and Ivujivik town-sites was circled, marking this as a limit on any future land selections. Second, Quebec inserted a clause into the agreement stipulating that, for communities that didn't select their allocated Category-1 lands within two years of the signing, Quebec would select their lands for them. For the communities that hadn't selected land, this was a menacing, heavy-handed threat made very real by being specifically stated in section 6.1.1 of the JBNQA.

Zebedee speaking his mind to Minister of Indian Affairs and Northern Development Jean Chrétien, Ottawa, January 29, 1969.

In a free democratic country, nobody should be forced to partake in anything they fundamentally disagree with. But events surrounding the James Bay court case had made Quebec hyper-assertive and determined to demonstrate its control over the 1912 lands. Quebec pushed its weight around like a ruthless dictator, exuding the attitude: "We'll show them who's Boss!"

For 38 years, Puvirnituq and Ivujivik had this ominous threat hanging over them. In 2015, Ivujivik finally signed on to the JBNQA and selected its Category-1 and Category-2 lands. As I write this, Puvirnituq is the only community that remains outside the JBNQA, still subject to the government's legal threats concerning land selection.

I have to mention the weakness of the federal government. Remember, the federal government held fiduciary responsibility for Indians and Eskimos since 1867. In essence, they had a duty to protect Aboriginal people from blatant exploitation and unjust treatment. What I saw in the James Bay negotiations was the federal government acting like the proverbial 98-lb weakling, incapable of coming to the defense of the Cree and Inuit. Ottawa was party to these negotiations, *only because it could not legally avoid being there.* It had tried to slough off its legal responsibility for Aboriginal people in its 1969 White Paper by proposing to transfer such responsibility to provinces. Not once in the James Bay negotiations did Canada stand up to Quebec and say, "You don't treat people this way!"

Not A Fix-All

In the years since 1975, some commentaries on the JB-NQA have ended with, "…here was another mistake/ shortcoming/omission of the Agreement." I don't often respond to such comments, feeling that responses ought to be provided by the surviving signatories as a group. My own knee-jerk response might go something like, "We didn't even have time to make mistakes!" Or, "The whole Thing was a mistake from which we merely managed to extract bits and pieces of benefit that prevented us from being totally flattened by James Bay."

The James Bay Agreement did not fix everything needed to make Northern Quebec a flourishing place on par with other Arctic regions of Canada. Not all of the major needs of our people and our communities were provided with resources, recognition, or remedy. The constant stress and high tension in the atmosphere of the negotiations made it impractical to devote "quality time" to all issues, including some that were of fundamental importance to Inuit.

In the Agreement-in-Principle of 1974, we managed to wedge in the need for Northern Quebec to acquire its own representation in Canada's Parliament and the National Assembly of Quebec, one of our objectives. We had diligently pursued this subject in our first formal sessions, but it was absent in the Final Agreement signed in 1975. This important issue was simply squeezed out by the sheer fullness of other priorities.

Another major issue not fixed to satisfaction was the status of the Inuktitut language. We achieved some minor provisions allowing Inuktitut to be tolerated and prevented from being pointedly disregarded if it appears beside the official languages, English and French. I've called such mentions *qinungajaugiikkutiit*, meaning "preventatives of overt scorn". Inuktitut's place is nowhere near the official status with attached adequate funding enjoyed by English, and yet the main justification by which we entered negotiations was our Inuit identity: our Aboriginality as distinctly separate from the Cree. The JBNQA didn't provide anything specific for the preservation of Inuktitut identity, language, and culture. This is sometimes mentioned as an oversight so obvious that the Inuit signatories can easily be blamed for not doing anything about it.

Apology and Wishful Thinking as "Philosophy"

No Cree or Inuit leader wrote an assessment of the James Bay Agreement to be attached to the final document. But John Ciaccia, MNA for Mount Royal and Quebec Premier Bourassa's Special Representative, made a speech to his colleagues in the Quebec National Assembly that was inserted in the front section of the Agreement. This speech revealed who presumed to be in the driver's seat of these negotiations, and made some amazingly pretentious statements.

The speech, entitled "Philosophy of the Agreement", was part apology for Quebec's long absence from the 1912 lands and part wishful thinking about "Cree and Inuit wanting to live in Quebec." It was a fully political rationalization for possession of the territory and its future. It had taken over sixty years for Quebec to get "on scene", but it wanted to clearly delineate its unquestioned authority over the northern territories as the main concrete result of these negotiations.

Mr. Ciaccia's speech is part of the historical record, and so is not open to belated editing. But some of his statements are half-cocked enough to require factual reality checks. Here is one fine example: "The Crees and Inuit are inhabitants of Quebec. They want to live in Quebec, to work in concert with the Government of Quebec, to be part of us."

I would add the word "involuntary" to "inhabitants of Quebec". No figure of authority in history had ever sought the consent of the Cree and Inuit to be placed in this jurisdiction called Quebec. I'd also pointedly question how Mr. Ciaccia concluded that, "…They want to live in Quebec."

My Takes On a Flawed "Philosophy"

John Ciaccia's "Philosophy" speech takes up the first twelve pages of the James Bay Agreement. But, it's merely one party's version of a multi-faceted narrative. None of the other parties to the agreement was asked to write essays. I cannot belatedly write an essay reflecting Inuit philosophy so many years after the fact. But I will offer my take on some of Mr. Ciaccia's statements:

He said: "The Agreement has enabled us to…affirm finally Quebec's presence throughout its entire territory."

My take: It has taken us 63 years to do. Since there is no logical explanation for this great delay, I won't dwell on this for very long. I'm just thankful that nobody else dwelled on this issue long enough to raise the possibility of the Government of Quebec being sued for 63 years of non-governance to this segment of its citizenry."

He said: "…there has been a cloud in this northern vision, and that cloud is the statute of 1912. The position of the native peoples was left unclear. It was our duty, the duty of the Government of Quebec, to clarify their position."

My take: It may seem a paradox to call the statute of 1912 a "cloud", it being our meal ticket to this great, expansive territory. As to our duty to clarify the native peoples' position, we've done our best to impress upon them just who is the Boss.

He said: "These people are inhabitants of the territory of Quebec. It is normal and natural for Quebec to assume its responsibilities for them."

My take: Herein lies a tale! During times of scarcity and hunger in the 1930s, the Hudson's Bay Company had extended welfare credit to Inuit, thereby serving a government function. The Company sent an invoice for these expenditures to the Government of Quebec, which refused to pay. Quebec cited section 91 (24) of the BNA Act, claiming these Inuit were "Indians" under federal responsibility. In 1936, the government of Quebec formally pleaded that a segment of its citizenry, living in the 1912 lands, was none of its business. It went to the Supreme Court of Canada, and won, in 1939, by having the Inuit declared a federal responsibility! Quebec's assumption of responsibilities for Aboriginal people in these lands has been far from "normal and natural".

Quebec's "philosophy", as expressed by John Ciaccia, conveniently overlooks facts of history; it is inconsistent with its declaration of smooth relations with the Cree and Inuit.

Contemplating Salvation of Culture

This paragraph from John Ciaccia's "Philosophy" statement deserves special attention:

> ...Quebec certainly has special reason to be sensitive to the needs and anxieties of population groups of a different culture who are in a minority position. And that is the position of the Crees and the Inuit. They are very tiny minorities. Their fate as collectivities would be sealed if the Government of Quebec were not determined to give their culture the chance of survival as long as it has vitality, and as long as they wish their culture to survive.

Granted, Cree and Inuit may be "very tiny minorities" in the big picture of the whole province of Quebec, but neither group carries a minority complex. We Inuit are overwhelming majorities in our respective communities. We have boldly stood up to resist government actions when our sense of identity is threatened. We have demonstrated such resolve during the Bill 101 crisis in 1977 and the sovereignty referendums of 1980 and 1995.

John Ciaccia grossly overstated this part: "Their fate as collectivities would be sealed if the Government of

Quebec were not determined...", etc. This assertion places the government in the position of supreme arbiter of life or death over Cree and Inuit cultures. Perhaps Quebec sees itself this way. But this totally discounts how intensely the Cree and Inuit value their own cultures and identities, and what they're prepared to do to prevent their "fate" from being "sealed". Here, Quebec expresses great generosity, "...to give their culture the chance of survival as long as it has vitality, and as long as they wish their culture to survive." We did gain formal recognition of our rights to hunt, fish, trap, and gather on the land and sea, without undue government regulation. However, such rights should have been acknowledged without any fuss by whichever "outside" authorities assuming jurisdiction over our ancestral lands, starting in 1670.

Now, hunting and fishing aren't the only substance of our culture. Our language, Inuktitut, is the foundation of our culture and identity. It has undergone systematic erosion in the past fifty-plus years, due to dramatic frontal encounters with civilization and modernization. Official languages, which are in no danger of disappearing, get plenty of help from public funding. Inuktitut will require deliberate, proactive help to survive. We could well take up Quebec's stated attitude of helpfulness to seek resources and recognition for Inuktitut's healthy future. This can happen through the instrument of Complimentary Agreements. As of 2016, there have been twenty-five such agreements, and we're counting.

More Gems of Quebec "Philosophy"

In reading Quebec's "Philosophy" statement embedded in the Agreement, one has to recall its disposition at the time the James Bay project was launched. Quebec had barged ahead to approve it without any regard for first dealing with Aboriginal rights, which were outstanding, written items in the boundaries extension laws of 1898 and 1912. Governments aren't illiterate, so one can suspect some deliberate intent about Aboriginal rights having been "overlooked".

One section of the speech is titled "No Paternalism", but the text is saturated throughout with self-congratulatory prose about Quebec's great generosity toward these "tiny minorities", the Cree and Inuit. We can try to plumb the depths of post-colonial ideology toward Aboriginal people as we read this:

> ...Quebec has rejected paternalism as a policy for dealing with the native peoples. ...The Government proposes to deal with the native peoples as full-fledged citizens. ...They are offered the services that are available to all other citizens of Quebec in their own communities. They are offered powers of local administration as great as those of other communities in Quebec.

Moreover, the Governments of Quebec and Canada will, for the purpose of helping them to meet their needs in the economic, social and community domains, allocate the sum of $225 million to 22 native communities in the course of the next 20 years. This sum cannot be distributed to individuals; it must be used by the communities.

Finally, and perhaps more important, the native peoples are offered a choice. They can be free, as individuals, to choose between their traditional occupations and new occupations.

...I think that both the Quebec Government and the native peoples can feel that they are sharing a victory. It is a victory for the Government, because, by virtue of the Agreement, the presence of Quebec is finally and completely asserted in the North. It is a victory also for the native peoples, because by the Agreement they are put on a new and more dignified footing, as a collectivity, than they have known in the past.

So, there's no paternalism? How wonderful! But we're never to forget that all good things flow from the government of Quebec! I've said this before, but I'll say it again: Quebec as a jurisdiction was merely catching up to provide its normal regular obligations to its northern citizens with services entitled to them. They didn't even need to do this through the instrument of an ethnic land claims agreement. The sounds of self-congratulation ring a little hollow here.

Rough-and-Tumble Imprints

From its beginnings to its legacy more than forty years later, the imprints of the James Bay experience have been rough-and-tumble, and hard-edged. This shouldn't be surprising; it was the product of warfare fought on many fronts. None of the Inuit veterans involved in this combat talk much about what they went through. But in recent years, whatever we share about the subject tends to focus on the negative, traumatic parts of it. The JBNQA was attained at very high cost!

Consider the following: Many of us were very young when we self-started our involvement in this issue. None of us had any idea about where it might end up. We forged an alliance with the Cree; the only people our ancestors had skirmished with around the tree line before Europeans became our common adversary. Our relations with the Cree were not always smooth and conflict-free.

We took on a court action against a sacred cow project that powerful forces in the country were forging ahead with. To some, going to court seemed to be lunacy. This included Inuit who had seen the early stages of project construction close-up. "It's hopeless to think you can stop this Thing", they said. But the path of least resistance, to do nothing, was not an option for us.

We truly pioneered a negotiations process, not just

The board of directors of the Northern Quebec Inuit Association (NQIA). 1975.
[STANDING LEFT TO RIGHT] Robbie Tookalook, Zebedee Nungak, George Koneak, Charlie Watt, Johnny Williams, Putulik Papigatuk [crouching] Sarollie Weetaluktuk, Mark Annanack, Peter Inukpuk, Charlie Arngak. Not present, Tommy Cain.

for being the first Aboriginal groups to enter into a modern treaty. We had forced Quebec, a decidedly unfriendly party, into negotiations that it would rather not have had to engage in. Also at the table were even unfriendlier titans of development, who considered their project a Holy Grail they could not be denied.

We did our best to defend Inuit interests under impossible conditions. Being forced through the hoops of extinguishment and surrender of our Aboriginal rights was heartbreaking. Having to accept small patches of ownership to land that looked like leftover cut-outs was soul-wrenching. Not attaining a real "government" was a non-success hard to swallow. To top it off, we earned the enmity of a sizable segment of our own fellow Inuit for our efforts.

The destruction of harmony among Inuit in Nunavik, which resulted from the James Bay Agreement, darkened whatever was gained for the Inuit through it. Verbal combat pitching Inuit against Inuit was the worst lasting by-product of the whole exercise. The after-effects of this animosity linger to this day and need to be squarely confronted, then soothed with healing, forgiveness, and reconciliation.

The Perfect Scenario?

When Inuit first entered the legal/political arena in 1972, some parties in the James Bay process practically asked, "Who are you? And what are you doing here?" Those who represented Inuit in this process, wrestled with colonialism on steroids. This was more than just a figure of speech. We had to shake Quebec out of the apathy of having been absent from the territory for sixty-three years. We had to continually prod Canada out of its self-proclaimed "alert neutrality", a euphemism for its preference to do nothing.

In the perfect "could've-would've-should've" James Bay scenario, one option could've been for Inuit to not sign that agreement! The extreme, irreversible extinguishment and surrender of Aboriginal rights shattered Inuit unity, at a terrible cost. In that event, Inuit would have hoped to achieve a deal better than what the Cree would agree to, at some indeterminate later time. This hope, however, would have to hang on the assumption that the powers-that-be would be agreeable to negotiating a separate, stand-alone agreement with the Inuit only.

Now, the Cree were the primary party in the negotiations. As such, their concerns were the primary focus of negotiations. Their rivers, hunting grounds, and trap lines were being blasted to bits, even while talks were going on. This put the Cree under almost impossible pressure to settle what they could within a timeline ruled brutally by ongoing construction on their lands. What we saw at close quarters through our interactions with governments and developers convinced us that there was unlikely to be a "better time" for negotiating...

Had Inuit withdrawn from the James Bay negotiations to wait for that "better time", the Cree agreement would've determined the Project's inclusion of the Great Whale and Caniapiscau Rivers, without Inuit participation. The Cree were going to settle for *something!* In that intense atmosphere, I recall a lawyer working for the Cree say, "If it comes to that, we will sign the 1974 Agreement-in-Principle as the Final Agreement!" No Cree leader really refuted that statement.

In the wait for that ideal nebulous "better time", one of the great issues to be resolved would be waiting for governments to stop demanding extinguishment and surrender as a precondition to negotiating land claims. On this subject, we would still be waiting for this to this day! Even constitutional recognition of Aboriginal rights in 1982 and the 2014 Supreme Court decision *Tsilqhot'in* have not erased governments' insistence on that extreme draconian measure.

In recent times, many First Nations groups have taken action to defend their rights in their *unceded lands* against developments that will damage their livelihoods and environments. Such groups challenge developers on the basis of not having extinguished or surrendered their rights. But governments and developers have no respect for the sanctity of unceded lands. Sometimes they send riot squad police units with snipers to deal with such groups – and this is 2017!

Healing and Reconciliation Needed

On March 27, 2014, almost 39 years after the signing of the James Bay Agreement, eight of the original eleven Inuit signatories met again in Ivujivik, at the Annual General Meeting of Makivik Corporation, the organization mandated to protect the rights, interests, and financial compensation provided by the 1975 James Bay and Northern Quebec Agreement. They had been invited to explain their roles and share their experiences in that life-altering event. There was much emotion in the air as these now-elderly men told their stories, recalling some especially painful events as if they happened yesterday.

These Inuit signatories were the first to cross the threshold that surrendered rights, which produced much unpleasant fallout, turning relationships among Inuit in Nunavik into a psychological and emotional war zone. The men who signed on to the Agreement endured withering ridicule from their own people for doing so. By contrast, in other regions of Arctic Canada, the Inuit who later signed land claims agreements suffered no reproach from their own people.

In Nunavik, criticism from dissidents went beyond slight internal opposition. Disagreements among Inuit became very public. Inuit signatories were treated as if they invented the evil deed of surrender and destruction

Zebedee signing the James Bay and Northern Quebec
Agreement, Quebec City, November 12, 1975.

of Aboriginal rights. The signatories were subjected to
verbal and physical threats from fellow Inuit who were
totally opposed to what they did.

The resulting whiplash from such vivid Inuit-on-
Inuit turmoil was to have long-lasting negative consequences. Most dissidents refused to take part in the
ratification vote, by which the James Bay Agreement
was approved. Two dissident communities closed their
schools for two years, as an expression of opposition to
being served by the Kativik School Board, an entity created by the JBNQA.

At the Makivik annual general meeting in March 2014
in Ivujivik, the surviving Inuit signatories called for a deliberate and formal process of healing and reconciliation

to reclaim Inuit harmony broken by the JBNQA. Such destructive forces had never before been known among Inuit. Even ordinary people engaged in heated arguments. Families and family clans supporting opposing sides were divided, seemingly beyond repair.

The signatories proclaimed it was time for former antagonists to forgive, heal, and reconcile with each other. They called for reconciliation processes to permanently lay these profound divisions to rest. Once this is achieved, they said, the next outstanding challenges for building up Nunavik can be tackled head-on with renewed energy – that of pursuing autonomous self-determination for Nunavik, coupled with finding the means for strengthening Inuktitut identity, language, and culture.

Long, Rough Osmosis

A Political History of Nunavik

PART 2

Lowering the Quebec flag. Nunavimmiut in several
communities protested Quebec's Bill 101 in 1977.
Courtesty of Avataq Culural Institute.

After James Bay, *Maîtres Chez Nous* on Steroids

The title of my story of Inuit involvement in James Bay is: "Wrestling with Colonialism on Steroids". As it turned out, Inuit soon had to take up a challenge much greater than fighting arrogant nationalists with a superiority complex. We eventually had to take on *Maîtres chez nous* on steroids: Separatism, a Quebec movement determined to carve out a country separate from Canada. It would include Cree and Inuit lands, with an administration that would inflict misery upon non-separatists.

When the separatist Parti Québecois first got elected in 1976, its leader was René Lévesque. This was the man who led Quebec's very first appearance in Nunavik 12 years earlier, as a Liberal cabinet minister. We quickly learned that Quebec nationalism and Quebec separatism were very close cousins. But pure separatism was not the first problem we had to combat. In 1977, the PQ government introduced its French language law, Bill 101.

Quebec's separatist government, acting in defense of its French majority, conceived a law that made French the only official language in the province. Inuit, also in defense of their own identity and language, said "NO!" to being forced by law to become francophone. They closed Quebec government offices, lowered the Quebec flag, and ordered Quebec civil servants to leave their communities as soon as possible.

But even separatists came to understand Inuit objections. They amended Bill 101 to accommodate recognition and exemptions for Inuktitut. The moral of this episode for Inuit leaders, present and future, is this: don't ever be intimidated by separatists and separatism.

NQIA annual general meeting, 1976.
The thick document on the home-made conference tables is the James Bay and Northern Quebec Agreement.
[LEFT TO RIGHT] Bobby Baron (with pen), David Okpik, Etua Putlayuk, and unidentified.

Referendums Upon Referendums

The Inuit record against Quebec separatism speaks for itself. Inuit strongly opposed the PQ project, but we are not simply anti-separatist and pro-federalist.

Quebec separatism is rooted in the historical tensions between the English and French in the "New World". These have included war, economic, and linguistic domination of the English over the French, and many other factors that only those who have been oppressed by such things can articulate. Inuit have had nothing to do with separatism's invention and existence; its substance and *raison d'être* is very distant from the Inuit consciousness.

But here's the kicker: If this project ever succeeded, Inuit would be primary victims of separation's practical effects; we would be citizens of a new country not of our choosing. This would be the fourth time in history that our citizenship status would change by processes beyond our control. We would be further isolated from our fellow Inuit in Nunavut and Labrador, scores of whom are relatives. It's not a stretch to imagine requiring a passport to visit fellow Inuit in those territories.

During the first Quebec referendum in 1980, the Inuit of Nunavik decided to hold their own referendum. This was done to provide a national profile for the Inuit position and to prove that Inuit leaders and spokespeople were not just mouthing-off their personal opinions about the subject. Inuit as a group may be insignificant in the context of French Quebec, but they occupy a great mass of land adjacent to the sea. Nunavimmiut voted overwhelmingly to stay in Canada.

Although actual terms of separation are never talked about during referendums, it's not a wild guess to assume that bodies of water that are now internal Canadian waters could become international waters. This would affect James Bay, Hudson Bay, Hudson Strait, and Ungava Bay. For Inuit, these are plenty of direct reasons to say no to Quebec separating from Canada.

Canada has tolerated a lot of misery from those promoting Quebec separatism. As if Canada can't take back the lands it gave away to Quebec in 1898 and 1912. I've often taken Canada to task for not asserting this possibility. The Inuit of Nunavik held another referendum parallel to the province-wide one conducted in 1995, and again proclaimed that they will not follow Quebec out of Canada.

Protesting against Quebec's Bill 101, Inukjuak Inuit close government buildings in 1977.

Two Outstanding Future Goals

The Inuit body politic in Nunavik was severely damaged by the divisions resulting from the James Bay Agreement. People were very close to being enemies. Life was fragmented and incomplete. For several years, with the exception of Co-op meetings, Puvirnituq and Ivujivik did not send representatives to any regional gatherings.

In 1983, when Premier René Lévesque offered to negotiate self-determination or self-government for the territory, he specifically stated that he would undertake this only on condition of "Inuit unity". But neither the leaders nor their respective bodies of followers seized this opportunity. Nine years after the JBNQA was signed, the divisions were still too deep, the scars too fresh, for Nunavimmiut to move toward reunification. The Inuit of Nunavik could not act upon the urgings of an outsider like Lévesque, even for a positive purpose. The work done later to pursue Nunavik government was undertaken in a unity vacuum. The enterprise became an exercise of trying to attain a "government" for the territory. Ten years of work toward this resulted in a proposal to amalgamate major public organizations as a prelude to negotiating a governing entity. This was put to a vote in a referendum in April 2011.

A majority of the people voted "no" to the amalgamation proposal. They just didn't see enough of a reflection of themselves in what was being proposed. Everything was just too public and non-ethnic! There was hardly a mention of the Inuit identity, language, and culture. "Inuit-ness" wasn't prominent at all in this initial design of a governing regime for Nunavik. Still, people are determined to enhance the quality of governance in Nunavik beyond what exists today.

Like finding unity among Nunavimmiut, the attainment of a "government" for Nunavik remains unfinished business. Those who take up this activity again would first have to seek a popular consensus on the project's exact objective and have it universally understood. A fundamental component of this consensus also has to include official recognition and resources for the preservation and strengthening of the Inuit identity, language, and culture. Fortunately, a clear blueprint for preserving the health of Inuktitut exists in a book, titled *Illirijavut: That Which We Treasure* (published by the Avataq Cultural Institute, 2012). This book contains five clearly articulated major recommendations, which the owners of the Inuktitut language have themselves defined as vital to the future of their Inuit identity. The desire to be self-governing is tied very closely to a desire for strongly maintaining the Inuit identity.

Conclusion: Permanent Alertness

The trials and tribulations of being Inuit in Quebec include more than occasionally being looked down upon by nationalist/separatist ideologues, some of whom actually believe that Inuit have no business asserting their identity in post-1912 Quebec. Such people act like they've always owned the place. They expect Inuit to be meek and docile, and to keel over without raising a fuss when Quebec politicians assert the realities and ambitions of their "nation": The language is French, the fight is with Ottawa, Quebec is a nation with its own predominant values. However, as French as Quebec is, it's impossible for Inuit to simply transform into becoming *"pure-laine Québécois".* Our ancestors didn't come from France. They weren't involved on the Plains of Abraham in 1759. For Inuit, sustained contact with French Quebec began only in 1964, practically yesterday.

We have endured Quebec's roughshod imposition of French names upon our lands and communities. We've had to fight vigorously for our rights over the James Bay Project. We've had to stand up to French being declared the only official language. We've demonstrated our opposition to separation from Canada in the referendums. Every once in a while, Quebec leaders make "steamroller" statements, seemingly designed to stress those who happen not to be French: "Anybody running for municipal office will have to be fluent in French. A Charter of Values will rule public institutions in Quebec. Separatism is here forever!"

Inuit spokespeople have had to clearly state their own truths without being intimidated by such pressure. A prominent Quebec bureaucrat once grabbed an Inuktitut newsletter from under my arm and asked, "*Well, Zibidii, what har you saying against us this time?*" I was delighted by this Big Shot reading Eskimo newsletters, and flattered that he paid attention to my opinions about Quebec…

It's unfortunate that defending Inuit interests in Quebec is often misconstrued as being somehow anti-Quebec. Inuit leaders have to be permanently alert to the twists and turns of Quebec's hegemony over Aboriginal people. Quebec politicians display no respect for Aboriginals when they go on their nationalist-separatist benders, when their French-ness is naturally supreme.

In my experience, the best defense against arrogant aggressive rhetoric is being intimately grounded in who you are, an Eskimo from a stock of people who've been here for thousands of years. Immigrant settlers and their descendants are not our superiors…